Beth Stephenson's

Americana

:

WITH GRATITUDE

To patriots who have sacrificed for their love of this great nation:
Both those who are known and those who are not.
ONLY IN AMERICA, GOD BLESS IT.

THANKS TO THE DAILY OKLAHOMAN FOR GIVING ME A
START AND TO MATTHEW PRICE FOR HIS EXCELLENT
EDITING AND OVERALL GOOD CHEER.

Beth Stephenson

CONTENTS

FORWARD

Forward

Years ago, I was conducting the music at church the Sunday before Independence Day. As I looked out over the congregation, I saw my brother, Mark, singing America The Beautiful in full-throated love and joy. My own voice caught and I could barely croak out the rest of the song. The hymn of patriotic love vibrated in my own heart, too. America is beautiful!

It would be many years before my husband, Jeff and I could afford to explore the nooks and corners of our national nest. But once we started piling our kids into the van, sleeping in campgrounds and budget motels, we were forever hooked..

Jeff loves to plan delightful itineraries, reveling in the diversity, beauty, history, cultures and customs different regions of our land have to offer.

I think I have visited every Civil War Fort and every major Revolutionary War battlefield in the country. I've visited all but two states and even some USA territories.

My national pride and love has only grown. Everywhere I go and even when I'm home, I find stories of kindness, courage and sacrifice, each adding a new color patch to the American crazy quilt.

The concept for *Americana* was born listening to the news. I was sick of the vitriol! Americans are not defined by their disagreements, but unified by a national culture of acceptance, neighborliness and family traditions. I realized that many of my fellow citizens either don't know or have forgotten all the amazing, delightful, breathtaking, heartwarming and courageous stories and scenes that reveal the truth about America.

Americana is currently published each week in The Oklahoman. It has steadily gained popularity as online 'shares' increase and fellow patriots catch the vision. Together we can make America even better by rejoicing in all that is good and great about this nation.

This volume is a collection of the first 52 weeks of published columns. It contains some heretofore unpublished photos taken by Jeff and me as well as some photos readers sent after reading the column. On some occasions, the column was edited by the newspaper to fit the space. This book contains the uncut versions. How grateful I am for a nation where we can write what we want to write, and say what we want to say without fear. It's one more thing that's great about this nation.

Only in America, God bless it!

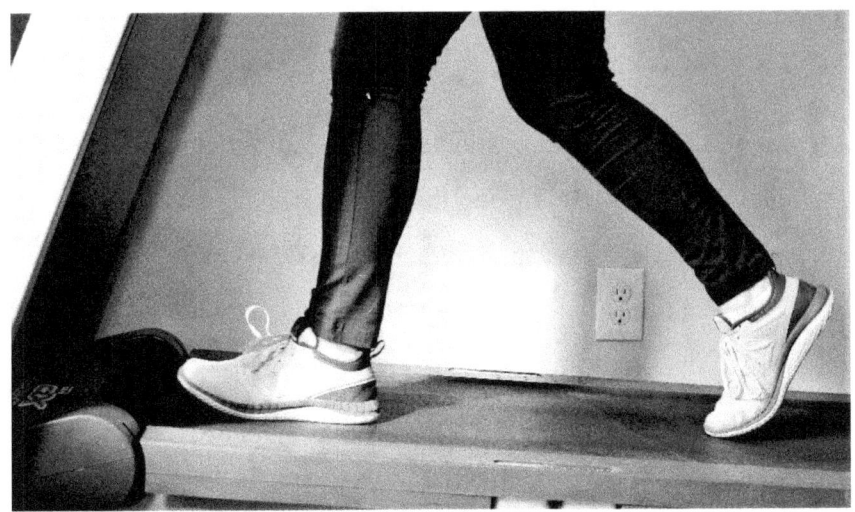

Chapter 1

Happy, Healthy New Year

Tis no longer the season of fudge and cinnamon rolls. The holiday treats have all become rolls around our waists. Tis the season of New Year's resolutions and taking the bad news from the bathroom scale on the (double) chin.

Many communities in the USA focus on exercise and health as a matter of civic interest. My brother Jim Mitchell owns an exercise facility in a chic little town on the coast of Oregon. Florence is nestled among fresh water lakes and broad sand dunes. Redwoods and pines thrive in the temperate climate. The ocean is bitter cold, but the lighthouses and pebbly beaches are calendar-worthy picturesque. Outdoor adventures abound. Exercise is part of the town's lifestyle emphasis.

All over the US, communities build hiking and biking trails and abundant sidewalks. But during the rainy winter, businesses like my brother's boom. Like many others across the country, Coastal Fitness offer tailor-made exercise routines to customers of different ages and limitations. Jim has a Master's degree in Exercise Physiology. His customers tend to be retirement age-ish and he offers some aerobic classes geared to his geriatric customers.

In world history, body fat equated with wealth. Now it's somewhat the opposite. In America, calorie dense and quick foods are cheap and abundant. Sedentary jobs are common in America as we use modern conveniences to do our physical work for us. Technology related jobs tend to keep our backsides planted in comfortable ergonomic chairs.

I don't live close enough to Jim to demand filial perks of free gym membership. So yesterday I spent several hours repairing the treadmill I haven't used for eight months. In truth, the machine has thousands of miles on it. My resolutions from the last 10 years have nearly worn it out. I'm hoping to eke out one more year of heart-pounding use.

Diet food companies, online weight and exercise monitoring businesses and exercise facilities gather new customers every New Year.

Millions of Americans will make a health improvement-related purchase this month. We fight the battle of the bulge because we enjoy plentiful food and physical leisure. Our very prosperity becomes a threat to our wellbeing.

I've made my resolutions. I'm not going to promise myself weight loss. I'm going to treat my body to plenty of exercise each week by enjoying the clean American air, the handy community exercise facilities, and my trusty (and recently lonely) treadmill.

Only in America, God Bless it.

Chapter 2

Buffalo National River

The unwanted Christmas gifts have been returned and we're all signed up for penance memberships with weight loss businesses. Yet our hearts tick the clock forward to the summer when the ice dams break and the rivers flow freely again. Our eyes grow hungry for the verdant greens of the warmer seasons.

Everyone has heard of National parks but it may be a different matter with National Rivers. The concept was new to me when Jeff announced that we were going to explore the Buffalo National River the summer of 2011.

It was easy to see why the NPS thought they needed a river to be part of the National legacy. In 1972, they designated the Buffalo River in Arkansas as the first fluid national park. It runs 130 miles generally eastward through towering limestone cliffs and dense woodlands. The national river area also includes strips of shoreline laced with trails.

Though the conditions change, the day we went, we had no concern carrying a toddler and some other young children on our tame floating route. Some of the adults were first-timers, too, so a seven-mile stretch was perfect for our pace.

There are several private companies that rent canoes or kayaks along the river. We rented canoes in St. Joes. The outfitter hauls the boats to and from the river in the places you designate. The day was hot and the temperature of the water was cool enough to draw a shout when I first dove in. Right near our put-in, there was a deep pool with an easily accessed cliff just above. Several of my family enjoyed showing off their daring by jumping from it.

There were fishermen all along the stream. Bass tantalized them, hitting the water and gliding deep again as we slipped over the surface.

Here and there a natural campground bore the marks of campfires. We were not prepared to camp along the river but the utter serenity of the place made me jealous of those who were.

We pulled onto the bank and spread our picnic beside a deep pool. After we ate, we swam and sunbathed for a while before we returned to the boats. Herons and hawks surveyed our progress. The woods are full of Hickory (wild pecan) Walnut, Elm, Birch, Oak and other species that I couldn't identify. The squirrels that scolded from the overhead branches were glossy and fat.

Though the website says that over 800,000 people visit each year, on the prime day for floating, the river wasn't crowded. Visitors are mostly respectful of the tremendous natural beauty and carry out anything they carry in.

During the civil war, nearby caves full of bat guano were mined for saltpeter to make gun powder. In 1863 Confederates had built a trim little settlement for processing the saltpeter, but the Union found it and burned it down. They took seventeen men prisoner and three others who were out cutting wood escaped.

There are several different float stretches, but there are also beautiful hikes along the river. Parts of the National River area include formal campgrounds and picnic facilities.

Every citizen in this nation owns a little bit of this beautiful place. It's a sampling of the best the Ozark Mountains have to offer.

Only in America, God Bless it!

Lunch Break on the Buffalo National River

Chapter 3

Honest Abe Lincoln

Inauguration Day and Martin Luther King Day fall in the same week this year. My thoughts turn to my favorite President of the United States of America: Abraham Lincoln. He wins that distinction from me because he knew that freedom was right and slavery was wrong and no political expediency caused him to dissemble.

Abraham Lincoln was a remarkably unsuccessful politician before the presidential election. He had been an Illinois State Congressman for 8 years, but was defeated for other offices he sought. His democrat nemesis, Stephen A Douglas, had courted Mary Todd (before she had become Mrs. Lincoln,) and they remained friends. Each political defeat threw Lincoln into deep depression that sometimes lasted months or even years. Douglas was again his opponent in the Presidential election.

Abraham Lincoln was 6'4" tall; Mary Lincoln was perpetually plump and 5'2" tall. Stephen A Douglas was 5'4". Lincoln's voice was high and nasal and Douglas's was deep and resonant.

Lincoln is purported to have told a story about a man who drew a pistol and waved it in Lincoln's face. Not wanting to ruffle his assailant, Lincoln asked how he had offended him. The man replied that he had made a vow that if he ever met a man uglier than himself, he would shoot him on the spot. To this Lincoln said he replied, "If I'm uglier than you, go ahead and shoot."

Ironically, Honest Abe was not a strict abolitionist. He believed that Americans of conscience must prevent the spread of the absolute evil of slavery into new territories and states. He expected that in the South, where slavery was deeply entrenched, it would die out on its own, without government intervention. His core belief was that good would triumph over evil because America was at its roots a righteous nation. His position shifted once the South declared war to defend the institution of slavery.

In the presidential election of 1860, Lincoln won the electoral college in a landslide, but garnered just under forty percent of the popular vote. Still today, he holds the record for winning the least percentage of the popular vote while still winning the election.The opposition vote was split between three candidates who were moderate to extreme slavery proponents.

Both Mr. and Mrs. Lincoln began receiving assassination threats as soon as the election was over. He wanted to avoid war and preserve the Union by any possible means without acceding to the spread of slavery. A brilliant orator, he regularly asserted that race was not relevant to natural rights.

The Southern Democrats had threatened for years to secede from the Union if a Republican (the abolitionist party), was elected to the presidency. About a month after Lincoln was elected, the South made good on their threat.

The day of his inauguration, there were no cheering crowds in (mostly Democratic) Washington D.C. Sharpshooters watched from every window along the route. The military escort shielded Mr. and Mrs. Lincoln from every angle. The citizens on the streets seemed openly hostile to the Lincolns.

Mary Lincoln found the White House in shabby disrepair. No first lady since Dolly Madison had taken much interest in maintaining the mansion. The $20,000 allotted for maintenance for each presidential term had gone unspent for years. Mary spent the cash in one shopping trip, replacing ragged carpets, window coverings and peeling paint. A notorious spendthrift, she bought everything she could find that would lend an air of opulence to 1600 Pennsylvania Ave. Her spending spree curbed only when the President threatened to pay for her purchases himself.

Raised in a wealthy Lexington KY family, Mary Todd Lincoln loved beautiful, extravagant clothes. Yet, she sometimes sewed for herself and her children and before going to the White House, did most of the family cooking.

The Lincoln's marriage is said to have been tumultuous and Mary Lincoln was known to deliberately embarrass the President if she felt slighted by him.

A month after the inauguration, the Civil War started when the Confederates fired on Fort Sumter, South Carolina. The President was adamantly against punishing the South once the war was won. When he visited hospitals, he is reported to have been equally warm and genuinely interested in the well-being of the men from either side of the conflict. He said that he was president over the entire nation, including those that disagreed with him.

He was assassinated shortly after his reelection and the end of the Civil War in 1865.

He dreamed of his own assassination shortly before it happened. I believe he would have freely given his life, had he believed it would seal his testimony against oppression and bondage in the hearts of Americans forever.

Only in America, God Bless it.

Chapter 4

Mystery of the Ancient Mounds

When I think of exploring ancient archeological sites, I think of the ruins in Rome, the pyramids of Egypt and Central America or the astonishing remains of Pompeii. Even the Anasazi cliff dwellings at Mesa Verde in Colorado seem mind-bogglingly old in our young nation.

But baking in the hot Mississippi sun and throughout the Mississippi River Valley there are numerous and widely scattered archeological sites, some that predate the cliff dwellings by a millennium or more. They are mounds, many shaped like pyramids with their tops lopped off.

Archeologists have determined that smaller mounds were used for burial of important citizens, chiefs and religious leaders. Larger mounds held adobe and wooden structures used as residences for the chiefs and possibly sometimes priests. Most were primary ceremonial sites.

The largest of these ancient mounds, the Cahokia complex in Illinois, is just across the Mississippi River from St. Louis. The Cahokia site dates to about 800 A.D. and at one time had a population of around 100,000.

The artifacts found in the ancient villages that surround some of the larger mounds, include evidence of human sacrifice, and cremation. Archeologists also recognize that the ancient peoples of America traded widely across the region. Copper spools and sheets of mica don't occur in Mississippi or Illinois and were imported from lands far to the north.

The National Park Service maintains many of these historic sites and they are free and accessible to visitors. Most known burial mounds in Mississippi date to the Middle Woodland times between 100 B.C. and 400 A.D. But early French explorers observed the Natchez Tribe still using mound sites for ceremonial purposes. They documented the mound-style burial of two important chiefs, Great Sun in 1728 and his brother, Tattooed Serpent in 1725. Valuable trinkets were buried with the honored dead along with his relatives and servants. (I wonder if the servant job application included that information.)

I visited one of the largest mounds near Natchez, Mississippi. It lies near the ancient roadway called the Natchez Trace which is an overland route that roughly parallels the Mississippi river. *TheEmerald Mound* takes its name from the 18th century plantation which surrounded it. It seems an apt moniker, considering the brilliant green grass that covers it.

The Emerald Mound is believed to be from the mid-Mississippian period in about 1250 A.D. The top of the mound is rectangular and spans about 8 acres. Archeology tools have proven that the mound was formed by lopping off the top of a natural hill about 30 feet above the forest floor and using the earth to fill in the sides to make it a rectangular pyramid shape. Another large mound rises thirty feet on one end of the plateau like bleachers above a stadium.

There were once a series of smaller mounds around the perimeter of the top of this mound, possibly forming a temple complex. But what archeologists call "rituals" or "ceremonies" today are called "sports." I wonder if they've looked for bags of popcorn and peanuts buried in the ruins of ancient concession stands.

We Yankees still have much to learn about the Land of the Free and the Home of the Brave. Many of those secrets may yet be locked in the ancient mounds of the Mississippi River Valley.

Only in America, God Bless it.

Beth Stephenson

Chapter 5

The Corps of Discovery

While the Mississippi River is the aortic artery of the USA, his cantankerous little sister, the Missouri River has almost an equally interesting history. Upstream on the Missouri River a few miles from St. Louis sits the charming little town of St. Charles. Since its founding in 1769, it has witnessed it's fair share of American history.

Thomas Jefferson, the third president, made the Louisiana Purchase. St. Charles was part of that purchase, acting as a gateway to the Missouri River. Early accounts suggested that the Missouri River flowed all the way to the Pacific coast. Jefferson's first priority was to try to find out what was in the grab bag he'd purchased and the Missouri River seemed the obvious highway.

He commissioned his friend, Army Captain Merriweather Lewis to head an expedition with a group of soldiers called the Corps of Discovery. The ostensible reason for the trip was to find a water route across the nation to the Pacific Ocean. The more subtle purpose was to establish in the minds of the many native tribes and even the French, English and Spanish that the new owners of the property intended to take possession. Earlier explorers and trappers had written that the Missouri River ran generally from North West to south east. While the Missouri River does travel farther west than any other river, they had failed to note that the Rocky Mountains prevented it from completing the liquid highway to the west coast.

Lewis was schooled by the funding organization, The American Philosophical Society and by Jefferson himself in preparation for the trip. He studied botany, geography, zoology, astronomy, meteorology, and other studies. He already had some knowledge of the use of a sextant for navigation. He chose his intrepid friend, William Clark, also an army officer, to be his partner in the expedition. Lewis spent hours studying in Jefferson's library at Monticello, reading reports from travelers and explorers that had traversed sections of the land.

The Corps launched in May of 1804, setting out on canoes and other shallow draught boats up the Missouri River. Lewis rendezvoused with Clark in the thriving burg of St. Charles Missouri two days later. The little town was already well established with comfortable inns and shops and was the easiest place to supply themselves with all the provisions they needed for the journey west.

Daniel Boone and one of his sons had established a permanent home near St. Charles in Defiance Missouri. As the gateway to the

wilderness, he combined the comforts of civilization with the adventure of America's natural wonders. Already famous as a woodsman and marksman, Lewis and Clark undoubtedly knew of him.

The Missouri is known even today as a treacherous water way with shifting navigation channels, shallow draught boats and canoes like Lewis and Clark's expedition paddled would not have been as troubled as later steam boats were.

Visiting St. Charles makes me think it must have been hard for those traveling west to leave the friendly streets behind. The wilderness would not return The Corps of Discovery for two years and 4 months.

St. Charles still thrives above the peacefully rolling Missouri. The historic district has been meticulously restored. The brick lined streets have upgraded to gas street lights since the days of Daniel Boone and Lewis and Clark. Restaurants offer old fashioned American menus as well as fare from its earlier cultures of French and Spanish. The tidy streets and historic buildings are scrupulously maintained. Historic inns have turned into Bed and Breakfasts and local shops offer antiques, books, confections, traditional crafts, collectibles and even Native American wares. Still serving as a gateway to discovery, the town has earned a reputation for being friendly to startup businesses. St. Charles has transformed itself from a point of departure into an interesting destination.

Only in America, God Bless it.

St. Charles, MO

Chapter 6

Attitude at Altitude

Election years are infamous for elevating squabbles to feuds and heightening concerns to horrors. If there were nothing wrong in the USA, there'd be nothing to fix. But politicians have to promise to fix something.

Happily, I'm not running for public office. As I travel all across this nation, from north to south and east to west, I delight in the diverse cultures that flavor our melting pot. I gawk at the majesty of America's scenery and I revel in the customs and cultures that flourish in their unique regions. I have no need to bring out the bad. *Americana* will wholeheartedly glory in the good in this great nation.

The wonders of America, both tangible and intangible are our heritage. She is us and we are her.

I just flew home from a funeral in Utah. My mother's

husband, "Grandpa Bud" died three months short of his 99th birthday, well-loved and loving to the very end. He was born during the first world war!

Somehow, my husband Jeff and I made it onto TSA's nice list. We didn't have to take the laptop out of its case or remove our shoes. A quick walk through a metal detector and we were good to go.

We did find a slip in Jeff's luggage telling him it had been inspected. I wasn't surprised. I can imagine the TSA agent staring at the X-ray, trying to figure out why Jeff had two insulated travel mugs, a pile of old CD's and a huge radio control car cushioned in dirty laundry.

The timing of Bud's death was ideal for our student son. The engine on his new truck had seized on Christmas Eve. We pitied him walking home from work at midnight in subzero temperatures and decided to take him the vehicle we weren't using. Even though we were flying home, we needed the Tijuana Brass, and an assortment of Broadway Musicals to get us through the long stretches where even evangelical radio doesn't reach.

The toy car was a gift from our son to his Oklahoma nephews. He hadn't considered how it would fit in a suitcase when he bought it.

But I wasn't thinking of the luggage as I waited in the TSA fast lane. I get nervous when people around me are asked to remove their clothing, especially their belts. Trousers' suspension is dubious enough on our well-fed American bodies without removing the safety device.

Like a game of Simon Says, nobody objects to their funny requests. We'd comply if they said to stand on our heads, do a pushup, turn in a circle: anything. We just hope our bland

expression will keep us from the dreaded pat-down search. I must have failed recently at the bland expression, since I was chosen for a wand search. They instructed me to hold my arms straight out, Simon says. An agent waved a wand over my body like Cinderella's fairy godmother. Nothing happened: no glass slippers, just men size 8 running shoes.

This time, as we approached the airport with my brother-in-law, Jim, he told us about a cute, plump, little lady at the Boise, Idaho airport on a recent flight he had taken. "She was about 70 years old, and we were chatting as we waited in the TSA line." he explained. She was asked to take off her shoes and her coat, but they still pulled her aside for a pat down search. They asked if she'd like the search to be done privately. The old gal told the agent, "Heaven's no! I want it out here where everyone can see! This is more attention than I've had in a while!" The TSA agent instructed her how to stand and she just kept grinning. As her generous proportions were calmly searched, she turned to my handsome, widower brother-in-law and winked. "This is more fun than I've had in years," she laughed. She apparently posed no threat to her fellow travelers since she soon trundled on her way.

An average of nearly 2 million people fly in America each day. The vast majority of travelers accept screening good-naturedly, even appreciatively. Screeners are friendly and polite. We move around this country in confidence, safety and peace, expecting and generally receiving prompt service and comfortable accommodations.

Only in America, God bless it.

Chapter 7

America's Mountain

I first heard the legend about the hymn "America the Beautiful" when we moved to the Colorado Springs region. The story goes that Katherine Lee Bates wrote the poem on top of Pikes Peak. I suspected it was false as soon as we passed the Pikes Peak highway toll booth. The Pike's Peak Highway rises like a spectre in my memory of dreaded, winding, guardrail-less roads. It twists around the mountain and vanishes into those "spacious skies." When we got to the top and I tried to stand up, my vision went dark and my head spun like something out of a horror movie. Did I miss the 'Bring Your Own Oxygen' memo?

My guests on that first visit are from the Portland, Oregon area. A daughter got out of our van and tossed her cookies into the weeds. Altitude sickness is like morning sickness causing vomiting, headache, fatigue, dizziness and general horribleness. For my youngest, it was several minutes before he could see anything. Another child's nose started to bleed.

So I knew that Katherine Lee Bates, an English professor at Wellesley College in Massachusetts, hadn't travelled two miles up from sea-level to compose sublime poetry. She was lucky if she had some dim memory of the "fruited plains" of eastern Colorado and Kansas stretched below her like a gold and green patchwork quilt.

The purple mountain magesties to the west line up like an assembly of rugged soldiers gathering behind General Pike.

The original version was called "Pikes Peak" and began, 'Oh beautiful, for halcyon skies.' 11 years later, the word 'halcyon' was changed for 'spacious' for the sake of us plebes that have no idea what 'halcyon' means. I looked it up. It's pronounced HAL-see-un and means 'tranquil' and 'prosperous'. I later learned that she wrote the poem from her room at the Antlers Hotel.

Zebulon Pike explored the region under the direction of Thomas Jefferson. He noted the easternmost fourteener, but got sick when he tried to scale it. I guess even famous explorers' bodies are partial to oxygen. Some compassionate fellows consoled him for his failure by naming the mountain after him.

The temperature drops about 50 degrees as you ascend. There's a donut shop at the top that makes a killing off coffee and hot chocolate. There's also a souvenir shop selling "Got Oxygen?" tee-shirts and other trinkets.

Humans make more red blood cells at high altitudes. The rangers

atop Pikes Peak seem to speak intelligently about the views and local flora and fauna. They could be marathoners in the kingdoms below. But there's not much that lives up there voluntarily. There are little ground-hog-like critters and some scrubby gorse shrubs.

Trees go nowhere near those altitudes.

On the way down, the smoke from burning brakes stings your nostrils until a ranger station arrests your decent . Someone takes your brakes' temperature. You can't go on until they have cooled to a safe range. Resist the instinct to set your emergency brake while you wait. It will warp your rotors.

The Pikes Peak Hill Climb is a 12 ½ mile race up the mountain each summer since 1922. It starts at mile marker 7. There's a $10,000 prize for drivers who navigate all 156 turns and an elevation gain of 4,720 feet averaging over 83 mph. I guess if you have nothing left to live for, it'd be fun.

Bates said she was thinking of Chicago when she wrote, "alabaster cities gleam." She had visited there on her way to teach summer school at Colorado College. I wonder if her heart leapt like mine docs when she first saw Pikes Peak rising like a star sapphire on the breastplate of America.

 The poet was born during the Civil war and in 1893 when the poem was written, the nation was still drying its human tears. Bates stated the American dream that some day it will truly be undimmed by human tears.

America, America, God shed his grace on thee
And crown thy good with brotherhood
From sea to shining sea.

Only in America, God bless it!

Chapter 8

The Freedmen's Bureau

Philosopher George Santayana is credited with saying, "Those who cannot remember the past are condemned to repeat it." But isn't history just proof that human nature doesn't change? There is nothing so universally abhorrent in our past that humans won't recreate it in a new style. I grew to love African American history as I researched a yet unpublished novel, "That Thy Days May Be Long." Here are some things I've learned.

It was illegal to teach a slave to read. Some learned naturally by paying attention to printed cues around them. In one slave narrative I read, a little slave girl was tasked with walking her white playmate to school each day and "forced" to sit with her while she did her reading, writing and cyphering, (arithmetic) homework. The slave was quickly much more learned than her mistress, though nobody taught her.

Slaves were forbidden to gather without white supervision. Consequently, they held midnight meetings in the woods to sing, pray and read from the Bible. Punishments for those caught holding a prayer meeting could leave permanent scars.

Black families were routinely separated. Since slaves could not enter contracts, marriages secured no legal rights to the couple or their children. Even marriages performed by a minister were strictly ceremonial. The tradition of calling adult slaves "aunt" or "uncle" probably stemmed from separation from biological families.

It was not uncommon for a slave to have a business as a tradesman in a different town from his or her master's home. He'd pay a flat tax to the master, usually 50%. After the Civil War, 4 million newly-freed slaves began their new lives searching for loved ones. Many had no homes, no marketable skills, no education and no money. The US government instituted the Freedmen Bureau to help slaves make the transition. Housing, employment, food rations, legal advice, and a method for creating a formal complaint were dispensed. The Bureau performed marriages, created health records and processed letters from slaves requesting help to find their families.

After 7 years, the Freedmen Bureau shut down. Soon the records were sealed in the National Archive. But now the Smithsonian

Museum of African American History and Culture will open late in 2016 and the Freedmen records have been reopened.

The Freedmen Bureau Project on FamilySearch.org is the process of transcribing the photographed Freedmen Bureau records posted on FamilySearch.org into a searchable database.

Anyone can do the 'indexing" and as a columnist and historical fiction writer, it felt like opening a treasure chest full of stories. One document was a labor contract for 15 men. They agreed to work from January 1 to December 31, six days a week. They were to be given "wholesome food," and between $10 and $15 per month, depending on the worker.

Another document was a complaint written in beautiful handwriting from a widow woman. She had left a "plantation" (farm) she owned in the care of a tenant for three months while she travelled to St. Louis. She went to nurse her only remaining son in a veterans' hospital. When she returned, she found that the tenant had filed an abandonment claim on her land so that he could take it over. She offered proof that the land was not abandoned and asked for redress of the declaration.

Another complaint tells of a blind man whose 5 children had been contracted to work in a neighboring county. 18 months later they were sent home without pay. He gave the address of the man who had hired them, but could not see that the recorder wrote the wrong state.

We don't know the end of the stories. Generations have passed. America still struggles to create an environment where the principles of freedom thrives and prosperity is available to everyone who is willing to do what it takes. But we've come a long, way from those dark days. Those ancestors held in bondage are being released from obscurity by research and technology.

 By bringing history to light, perhaps we can avoid at least the worst sins of our American past. Still when the sweet chariot swings low for me, I'm going to have lots of questions on the other side.

Only in America, God Bless it!

A Freedman Bureau School with its teachers and pupils

Photo sent by reader Greg Lewandowski. Taken at Edwards AFB

Chapter 9

Where the Land Rumbles & the Sky Goes Boom, Boom

I didn't get the joke when as a teenager my family moved from the coast of central California to a St. Louis neighborhood. "So you're from the land of fruits and nuts?"

"Oh yes. We had an acre of apple trees."

They'd grin.

Years later, I found myself back in California. My husband and I had four children by the time my husband's work transferred him from the San Joaquin Valley to the Los Angeles office. Our rental house was 30 miles from his office and his commute was about an hour and a half.

So we moved to the high desert of Los Angeles County: twice as far, same commute time, cheaper housing.

The Mojave Desert is not the first thing that comes to mind when you think of California. Our new home was delicately called a "fixer."

The day we moved in, the children dragged me urgently out back.

A 3 inch dead scorpion lay on the patio. They were thrilled! The unfenced backyard opened onto a space that would have been called a field if there'd been any flora. Beyond that, bicycle tracks marked suicidal hills suggesting future delights.

The neighbors' oleander bushes bloomed over their block walled backyard. The children boosted each other to peep at their green lawn and orderly blooms. "We have a lot more sand than they do," they proudly announced.

Inside, the peeling green linoleum and tattered brown shag made me sigh.

Our yard eventually bloomed and we put up a fence for the children to climb over. Tile replaced the linoleum, and our new tan carpet seemed impossibly chic.

We grew to love our desert home. It had only one fault. Some geologist had named it 'San Andreas'. Later studies of a reliable map showed it ran between our living room and family room. Real estate agents said that it was better to be closer to the fault than farther away because of the shape of earthquake shock waves.

Did you know that every canine and coyote howls before an earthquake? Next, you hear a deep rumble calling you to repentance. A unique vibration sets you to shaking an instant before the earth follows suit. We had only two minor earthquakes in the 40 months we lived there. They're still waiting on the 'big one.'

Almost every evening, the sky would explode in color like the angels took target practice in a paint store. In the spring, those reds, oranges and purples bend down from the sky to lick the Antelope Valley in a wildflower Mardi Gras. Poppies, primroses, lupine and aster blanket the desert in a crazy quilt of color. Hundreds of people drive into the wilderness as we did, to revel in the desert's redemptive transformation.

Nearby, Edwards Air Force Base welcomed home Space Shuttles with their double sonic booms. BOOM! BOOM! The space shuttle has entered the atmosphere! Most of the runways at Edwards, including the ones where the space shuttles landed, are unpaved, dry lakebed, naturally flat and desolate.

One morning in early summer, I dragged my kids out of bed before daylight to drive out to Edwards AFB to watch the space shuttle land. By 6 a.m. thousands of cars lined the dusty roads. We parked with a clear view of the shuttle hangar with the landing strip vanishing into the north.

My hungry, chilly children struggled to appreciate the charm of a view of witchy Joshua trees through a galvanized chain link fence. We waited in the car as the day warmed.

BOOM! BOOM! We flew back to the fence. America had already lost Challenger. We were silent with sudden dread. Heat rose in ripples from the runway.

We did have a great view of the hangar. But the space shuttle touched down several miles north. "That was about as exciting as tossing a piece of rice in the air," my daughter Tricia commented.

The littler ones missed it altogether. Eventually, Columbia rolled into clear view, safe, sound and triumphant from the abyss of outer space. So what if we didn't see the moment of touch down? It was still a wonder: a modern miracle.

Only in America, God bless it!

Photo sent by reader Greg Lewandowski. Taken at Edwards A

Chapter 10

Cajun Country Swelters in Kindness

New Iberia is a little town in south central Louisiana where they bottle heat. It is the caldera of chili sauce, a gastronomical wonder guaranteed to simmer your innards for days.

But it was 'Shadows on the Teche,' an antebellum mansion, that drew us to the sweltering little town. The spreading oaks are clothed in tattered Spanish moss. Hollyhocks and poppies splash the whitewashed fences with color.

The day we visited, we also entertained the hope of finding someone who could replace a rotten fuel line on our rattletrap RV.

Incidentally, the word 'antebellum' means 'before the war,' and is usually used to mean 'before the Civil War.' The word 'mansion' means 'much bigger than an ordinary house,' which definition seemed loosely applied in the case of "Shadows on the Teche." But the wonders of hyperbole (pronounced hyper-bully and meaning extremely bully) had imbued the old house with grace and honor enough to please me. 'Shadows' had all the white columns, and trim shrubbery a history lover requires.

 The Bayou Teche is believed to be the original course of the
Mississippi River but because of deltaic switching, a process of
filling up a riverbed with silt and debris until it changes course, the
Teche is now little more than a stream of tobacco juice drooling
down Louisiana's chin.

In a slave inventory made in 1839 by 'Shadows' owner David
Weeks, he lists: "A Negro man named Frank aged about 50 years
and his wife named Martha aged about sixty years valued at four
hundred and fifty dollars.
"A Negro man named Isaac aged 35 years and Louisa his wife
aged about 24 years with their Eight children." He gives their
names and values the family at $3,700. Policy at 'Shadows' seems
to have been to keep slave families together. Their main crop was
sugar.
 Nowadays, New Iberian farmers distill chilis into liquid fire. With
temperatures in the hundreds and humidity similar, the chilis cook

themselves in heat they collect as they ripen. Tourists ripen as they
cook.

After our 'Shadows' tour, the friendly docents listened to our tale
of motorhome woe and directed us to Dugas Auto Repair.

The proprietor welcomed us like family, even giving us the keys to his truck so we could see the sites while we waited on the repair.

Still, we were mildly uneasy. He dismissed our request for an estimate saying they didn't usually work on motorhomes . He quickly introduced us to a mechanic wearing a cotton work shirt with "Boo" embroidered on his chest.

Boo's shirt looked like he'd been swimming when he finished the fuel line several hours later. He explained he hadn't wanted to run down our battery with the air conditioning.

The owner made out the bill. It was less than half of what we expected. The owner shrugged off our gratitude. "We're glad you came to New Iberia," he said. "Come back soon."

We asked Boo if we could take his picture. In his thick Louisiana accent, he said he was "camera shy, bein' all dirty and sich," but he let us take it anyway.

The Motor home is long gone, but the photo is a family treasure.

Only in America, God Bless it!

Shadows on the Teche

Chapter 11

Wild Horses

My first full length novel was based on the life of my co-author's grandfather, Rasmus Anderson, a bona fide Mormon Cowboy. Just 150 years ago, he made his living herding wild mustangs in the mountain west. The stories of stitching wounds with horsehair and setting bones were enough to turn any urbanite pale. The heroes of western movies are spit shined and far more glossy than reality.

I wonder what OSHA would say to a boss who rousted his employees before daylight to gallop headlong over uneven territory, driving wild horses into a box canyon. They'd sleep on the ground and had nowhere to bathe. Once they got the horses penned, they'd build a fire to heat the branding irons. I wonder what PETA would say about the cowboys tripping the horses with a noose around their ankles and then pressing a searing brand into their rump or shoulder.

We're not talking about a few strays for stealthy Indians to creep up on in a western movie. Hundreds of wild horses herded together, led, not by the irritable stallions, but by bossy mares.

Adolescent mustangs, (what they were, not what they drove,) ranged around the periphery, bloodied by the fathers of the pretty fillies they attempted to steal. When the mares said 'move,' the herd followed.

The mustangs are mostly gone now. There are still herds wreaking havoc in parts of Nevada and other areas in the Mountain west. In fact they still plague the nearby communities by overgrazing if you let them. My horse husbandry experts explain that horses like to stand still to graze so the grass is bitten off over and over again in the same area. Bovine species like bison and cows move around as they graze and are much less likely to damage the range they live on.

2000 miles to the east, the descendants of equine Spanish shipwreck survivors cool their hooves in the surf of the Outer Banks of North Carolina. The horses wander the sandy islands, displaying their ribs under their shaggy coats.

We vacationed one summer on the Outer Banks. The house Jeff rented was accessible only with a 4-wheel-drive vehicle over a roadless beach. It was better to be there before high tide.

Our first morning, we carried the sea kayaks that came with the rental over the dunes to the beach on the Atlantic side. Metal signs warned not to touch, feed or disturb the wild horses, promising the disobedient penalties to make a terrorist quiver. But I wonder why, since the horses are obviously a non-native species. Are vegetarians a protected class or is it just their sheer coolness that garners special government protection? I could build a political campaign around that question.

Coolness aside, it seems to me that anyone foolish enough to put their tender bodies in reach of the powerful hooves and teeth of a wild horse deserves whatever they get. We obediently paddled boats into deep water or pitched ourselves off boogie boards to avoid cracking up against their wandering legs.

North Carolina horses form micro herds, each with a protective stallion, an alpha mare and a brood of prepubescent foals and lesser mares. Similar to their Nevada cousins, bachelor groups orbit around the central herds, even though they neither are, nor own mustangs.

Later, when we took the canoes out on the sound side of the island, we met lone horses standing thigh deep in the brackish (meaning slightly salty) water, grazing on the sea grass. These southern horses politely nibble . The underwater grazing keeps them from damaging the forage. They also eat sea oats and any other green thing they find.

I love to ride horses bareback but I'm afraid of the threats on the signs and I don't enjoy being bucked off. So I'll never mount a wild steed and feel the salt air whipping back my hair as we gallop in the sandy surf. But the wild horses are still there, taunting me for my cowardice. May it ever be so.

Only in America, God Bless it.

Wild horses on the beach in the Outer Banks, NC

Chapter 12

Concord: Grapes, Guns, Writers, & Hippies

There's a tree-shaded town of gardens and gables in Massachusetts named Concord. It's the place where in 1849, Ephraim Bull developed the Concord grape. He planted 22,000 test seedlings before succeeding with a richly flavored grape that ripened before killing frosts.

Those who disdain purple mustaches know Concord for the place an errant soldier fired a shot heard round the world, thus tipping the domino toward American Independence.

My childhood favorite author lived in Concord. Louisa May Alcott, wrote *Little Women* and each generation of little women since then weeps over the words, "the grass was already green over her sister's head." My name is taken from that book.

Tours of the Alcott home are a bit pricy and since the men in our family aren't interested in writers of books like *Little Women,* we compromised for a visit to the Old North Bridge that melting hot day, where we got a scintillating description of the first battle of the Revolution.

By the mid 1800's, Ralph Waldo Emerson was all the rage. When his first wife died, he forsook the ministry and Christianity to develop the original hippy movement. He called it 'Transcendentalism,' asserting that God is nature and nature is God. The movement urged a vegan diet, using no leather, no wool, and enslaving no man or beast. Emerson claimed his central doctrine was the "infinitude of the private man."

Critics called transcendentalists 'anarchists', but the rhetoric was catchy enough to make Emerson the father of the lucrative lecture circuit. He lost his mental abilities in his mid-sixties, but nobody hints that his condition was tied to Ephraim Bull sharing grape juice left too long in the sun.

Louisa May Alcott's father, Bronson Alcott undertook to start a Utopian commune based on his neighbor's Transcendental principles. Alcott refused to 'enslave' animals for farm work. Yet gossips observed that when the heavy labor of farming was needed, the intellectual founder was found elsewhere. His daughter

Louisa May remarked, "The band of brothers began by spading garden and field; but a few days of it lessened their ardor amazingly."

After seven months and a threat from his wife, Alcott commented, "None of us were prepared to actualize practically the ideal life of which we dreamed. So we fell apart". Since they ate no dairy products, was it from osteoporosis?

Nathaniel Hawthorne, author of *"The Scarlet Letter,"* sometimes penned his stories just down the street from the Alcotts and Emersons. Thought haughty by some contemporaries, his friends excuse him as shy. Hawthorne was too skeptical of human nature to fully embrace Transcendentalism.

Not true of Henry David Thoreau who embraced its concepts of freedom from responsibility with delighted abandon. Often in debt, he lived "freely" off (Emerson's) lakefront land and the largess of his enterprising friends. His book *Walden* poetically dispenses pithy bits of witty wisdom as Thoreau extols the freedom of owning nothing, living entirely for personal gratification and shows why he never had a wife.

But Thoreau could make a little go a long way. He was arrested for owing 7 years of back poll taxes. He spent the night in jail, was released the next day after his aunt paid his tax and wrote the acclaimed *Civil Disobedience* of his experiences 'in prison.'

But my most compelling memories of Concord involve neither grapes nor battles, hippies nor writers. It's ice cream! Oh the ecstasy of dipping a spoon into softball sized scoops of coconut chocolate almond with lava flows of hot fudge and nuts wearing top hats of whipped cream! Nobody could apologize better for the fierce Concord summer than a Kimball Farm banana split.

I wonder if Kimball Farm had been in business all those years ago, would any soldier have thought his life so cheap as to risk missing a sundae waiting five miles to the north? Would the Transcendentalists have changed their creed to include dairy and thus not "fallen apart?" Maybe the authoress would have been too cheerful to kill off her dear little Beth.

Indeed, a small helm turns a great ship.

Only in America, God bless it.

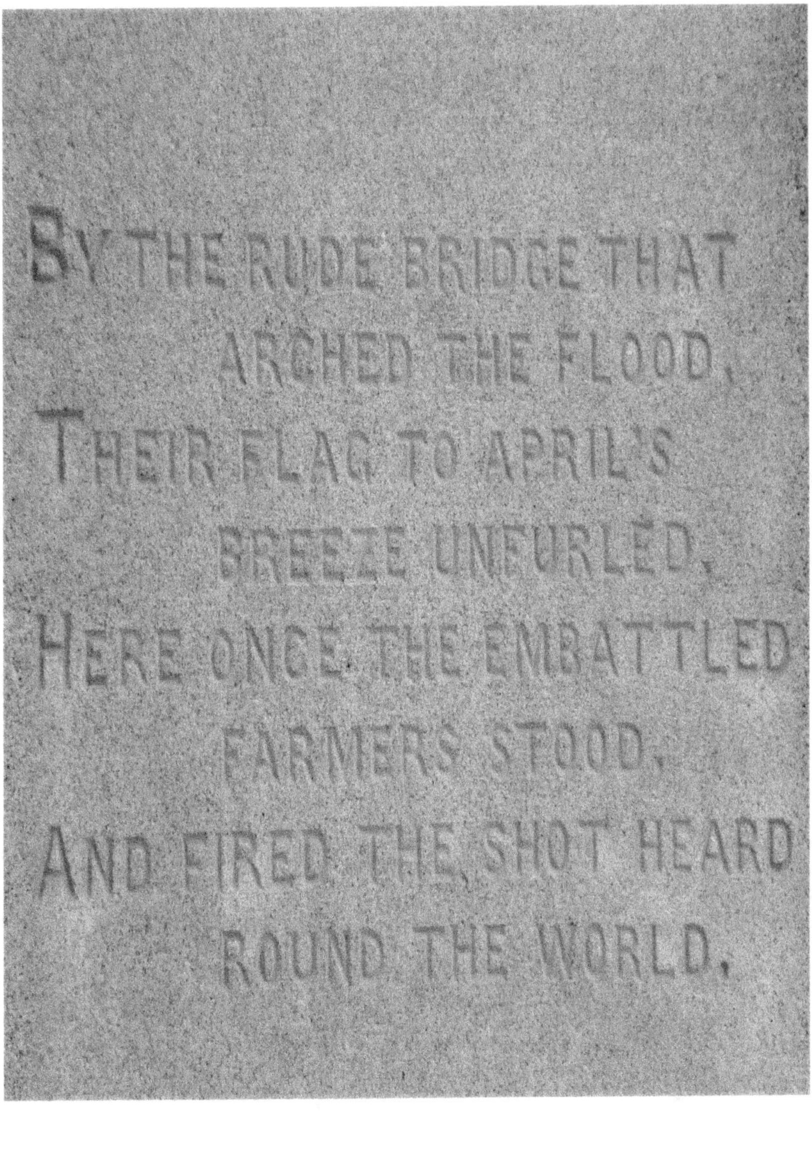

BY THE RUDE BRIDGE THAT
ARCHED THE FLOOD,
THEIR FLAG TO APRIL'S
BREEZE UNFURLED,
HERE ONCE THE EMBATTLED
FARMERS STOOD,
AND FIRED THE SHOT HEARD
ROUND THE WORLD,

The Old North Bridge where the shot heard round the world was fired

The Minute Man Statue near Concord

Beth Stephenson

Chapter 13

Anasazi Cliff Hangers

Long before Columbus was a twinkle in his father's eye, Americans were tucking elaborate apartment complexes into the shallow caves of the southwest region. Villages hung suspended on the lower lips of vast cliff faces in Mesa Verde and other sites in the Four Corners region.

Many of the cliff villages are accessible only by steep ladders or even ropes. While archeologists believe that they built in those highly inconvenient and dangerous places for the sake of defense, I have a different theory. I think either it was the ancient people's way of helping natural selection weed out the klutzes or there was a dominant gene for real estate salesmen superstars.

The cliff dwellings blend with the rock faces like crows feet on a smile. From the vantage point of a canyon rim opposite, if not for the black, rectangular or T-shaped windows, they'd be all but invisible.

The dwellings are stacked like children's building blocks, with short, narrow doorways, and dark, closet-sized rooms. Storage areas sometimes carved from the native stone line the back with dark passageways traversing the innermost edge of the ceilings and cave walls.

Though some of the pueblos had seeping springs bringing snow melt and rain naturally into the cliff villages, others were forced to descend the cliff face to bring water from a stream on the canyon floor.

There's no reliable source of food on the ledge of a cliff and the Anasazi couldn't all live in the village. The cliff dwellings were perhaps a place of resort in danger. In Mesa Verde, they had subsistence farms on top of the mesa where they grew beans, corn and squash. They are also thought to have hunted, gathered and raised livestock.

In modern times, rangers tour visitors through cliff dwellings like Mesa Verde National Park, explaining the social, economic and spiritual lives of those who once lived there. Most of the ancient ruins have at least one kiva, an underground structure with a specific pattern of construction, depending on the era when it was built. But the things that are known certainly are enough to surmise much more.

Only males over a certain age were allowed in the kiva. But the thought of descending into a smoke-filled room packed with teenage boys and men who had no ready access to bathing, hints that the women probably didn't mind the ban. "No honey, you go along to your man-fest. I'll just stay up here in the fresh oxygen grinding this corn with my stone pestle while I watch for invaders."

But invaders would have it hard. As soon as an enemy dropped into view on the village ladder, the closest native could push the ladder into the abyss and invasion was over.

Then again, one enemy with a sturdy club sitting atop the ladder could lay siege to an entire village. The cliff villages were part of larger social networks, but it's really hard to get reception from the face of a cliff to call for help. They must have been expert preppers.

The films in the National Park visitors' centers imply that the Anasazi disappeared mysteriously. But what's the mystery? I expect researchers to eventually come across a record sealed in a stone box that starts, "I was too tired to work the day of the BIG wind. . ."

Just climbing the ladder from one of the sites was enough to shiver me timbers.

Truthfully, starting in the mid 1100's there was a three-centuries-long drought that weakened the people of that desert region and eventually forced them to relocate to more hospitable areas. There is also evidence of them changing their religious forms to appease the offended climate change gods.

Anasazi beans are descendants of beans found in the ancient dwellings. But they taste like and have the same effect as their common bean-cousins. Did I mention that the kivas had no ventilation at all?

Even the word, 'Anasazi' is politically incorrect. Commonly understood to mean "ancient people," it's actually a Navajo word meaning 'ancestral enemies.' So I deserve a peace prize for serving Anasazi beans on a Navajo taco.

Only in America, God bless It!

A Park Ranger leads visitors to a ladder in Mesa Verde National Park

Chapter 14

Won't You Be My Neighbor?

The first thing on my email this morning was a note from a neighbor to everyone in the neighborhood. Apparently, there was a prowler, dressed all in black, skulking between the houses near the neighborhood entrance. The neighbor was out jogging before 6:00 a.m. and noticed the person. He yelled a greeting, in case it was a homeowner wandering outside in black pajamas, but the individual slunk behind one of the houses.

The report of a potential burglar, rather than causing fear, made me grateful. Bless the man who rises just after 5 each morning to exercise and at the same time to patrol the neighborhood.

Another neighbor collects trash as he jogs, keeping this whole area in and around our neighborhood free of litter. Once he almost mistook a $100 bill caught in the predawn breeze as a piece of trash. He earned wages for his good work, that day.

There is a little boy with Down's Syndrome who's always good for a smile and a wave. Another little boy calls me "Miss Beth" in the charming southern style. He asks how I am and wishes me a good day.

I realize that dogs gotta do what dogs gotta do, but I greatly appreciate that their owners take care of the doo. It's part of being neighborly.

One day, a house security alarm was blaring every few minutes. Several near neighbors assembled. One called the owner. Another walked the perimeter to be certain that it was a false alarm. Before the fire department could respond to the monitored system, the neighbors had seen to the safety of the property.

When we go out of town, all of our near neighbors keep an eye on our home. They water the porch plants and carry in any packages that might be delivered while we are away.

When a neighbor died, the neighbors inundated the grieving family with meals. It probably wasn't really needed. But the impulse to express concern and interest in those around us is part of being a good neighbor.

I know that life in the suburbs is not for everyone. Not everyone enjoys raising a flower or vegetable garden. Not everyone wants a quiet place to walk in the fresh air. But the feeling of

Neighborliness is not limited to my type of neighbors.

When my potatoes rolled off my grocery cart without my noticing, a kind man carried them to my car for me. Another lady in the grocery store told me the secret to scoring great deals on meats. A lady at the car dealership where I was waiting for a recall to be serviced shared a chapter from a humorous book she was reading and another told me where to get free snacks from the dealer.

Caring for those around us is part of American culture. Protecting the vulnerable among us is part of who we are as a nation. Neighborliness spins the very thread of which Old Glory is woven.

Only in America, God Bless it!

Valley Forge Cabins were built to precise dimensions. Soldiers competed to finish their shelters first.

Chapter 15

Valley Forge Leaves Lasting Impressions

Valley Forge, Pennsylvania is now a peaceful sea of waving grass painted with wildflowers and dotted with grazing deer. The cabins returned to nature. The ridges of the earthen redoubts and redans have softened with time.

Set aside in 1976 as a National Historical Park, Valley Forge is a place to remember the cost of freedom.

The Schuylkill River (pronounced skool-kill) flows past one side of the 3,500 acre site of the Continental Army's winter encampment of 1777-78. The river empties into the Delaware in Philadelphia 20 miles away. The American capitol was occupied that winter by the British.

Now there are a few replica cabins placed around the park for effect. Each 12' x 14' structure housed 12 men.

The Continental Army was ill fed, clothed and short of

ammunition, to say nothing of being poorly trained, when they entered Valley Forge. Of those 12,000 men, only 8,000 were left by June. 2,000 had died from diseases such as Typhoid and Typhus or exposure. Contagion spread readily in crowded cabins. Desertion accounted for the rest of the missing.

Their commander was General George Washington. He begged the Continental Congress for support for the hungry, freezing men. But Congress deadlocked for months quibbling over how to fund and feed the army. Many were dissatisfied with Washington's leadership. Some argued to unseat Washington, angry over the army's defeats in battle.

Meanwhile, Washington ordered the men to build cabins of native timber and mud. Though he had rented a comfortable farm house on the edge of Valley Forge, he refused to move from his tent until the last soldier was housed in a cabin. It was late February.

Washington was grief-stricken when he learned of the plot to unseat him as commander. He commented that if the Congress was dissatisfied with his leadership, he would return quietly to private citizenship. His humility and hotly loyal friends in Congress eventually deflated the opposition and the "cabal" against him dissipated. Supplies began to flow into Valley Forge more steadily.

Prussian military leader, Baron Friedrick Wilhelm Von Steuben joined the camp at about the same time. Though Congress would not commission him at first, he joined Washington as a volunteer and received authority to train the soldiers. The Baron spoke German and wrote his training instructions in French to be translated and copied. The handbook that resulted was the US standard through the War of 1812.

The soldiers that stayed in Valley Forge through the winter emerged as a well-trained fighting force. They had never heard of 'Constitutional Rights.' There was no guarantee of success. They risked everything to establish a nation where men would be free of oppressive government and flourish from their own effort.

The battle for freedom slowly turned in their favor. Eventually, victory justified the sacrifices of the freedom fighters and today, the gentle breeze stirs the Stars and Stripes over Valley Forge.

Only in America, God Bless it!

Dirt mounds insulated the cast iron bake ovens used by the Continental Army at Valley Forge

Chapter 16

Oh, Say Can You See

The biggest flag I'd ever seen welcomed me to the Smithsonian Museum of American History. It was the original Star Spangled Banner, then tattered and dirty: 30 feet tall and 42 feet wide. Each of the remaining stars and the stripes measuring about two feet across.

Historians attribute the design of the original American flag largely to George Washington. It is uncertain whether Betsy Ross really made the first flag. She is credited with convincing Washington that by clever folding, an easier to stitch, symmetrical 5 point star could be made with two scissor cuts. He wanted to use a six point star of David.

But The Star-Spangled Banner is not the original flag. An experienced flag maker named Mary Pickersgill and several assistants were commissioned to make a garrison flag to fly over Fort McHenry at Baltimore, Maryland. The flag's body is made of loosely-woven wool and the stars are made of cotton.

The story goes that an amateur poet named Francis Scott Key was held prisoner on a British ship overnight as the walls of Fort

McHenry were bombarded in the War of 1812. He waited for the "dawn's early light" to see if the American flag still flew over the fort or if the British Union Jack had been raised over a conquered Baltimore.

In the first stanza of his poem, he asks the question, "Is it still there?" In the second verse, (that never makes it to the sporting events or the graduations) he answers. "Now it catches the gleam of the morning's first beam, In full glory reflected now it shines on the stream; 'Tis the star-spangled banner!"

The Star-Spangled Banner started out with 15 stars, up two from Washington's original 13, for Vermont and Kentucky. After all the trouble and expense Thomas Jefferson went to to secure the Louisiana Purchase, one owner of the Star-Spangled Banner casually snipped a star out, (Kentucky?) and gave it away as a souvenir. Kentuckians have an excuse to feel insecure.

A later owner casually stitched her first initial onto a stripe.

When I first saw the famous flag in the Smithsonian the year after this nation's bicentennial, it had been patched, reinforced, stitched to a linen backing and hung vertically for the public to admire. In

2000, restorers painstakingly clipped over a million stitches to free it from the backing, cleaned the fabric and attached it to Stablitex, a lightweight polyester material. It's now reclines almost horizontal in a climate controlled chamber.

The third stanza of Key's poem is too unfriendly to be widely sung these days, referring to the old world oppressive government as "foul footstep's pollution." But the prayer in the fourth verse of the poem that would become our national anthem tugs my heartstrings. "Oh, thus be it ever, when free men shall stand, Between their loved homes and the war's desolation! Blest with vict'ry and peace, may the heav'n-rescued land Praise the Pow'r that hath made and preserved us a nation! Then conquer we must, when our cause it is just, And this be our motto: "In God is our Trust!" And the star-spangled banner in triumph shall wave, O're the land of the free and the home of the brave!

Only in America, God Bless it.

Chapter 17

Juneteenth, A Holiday You May Not Know

Last year, I spent Juneteenth , June 19, in Galveston, Texas. The year before that, I spent July 4 in Philadelphia, Pennsylvania. If it seems like a non-sequitur, it's not.

Truthfully, until I learned about the Freedmen Bureau Project, I'd never heard of Juneteenth. Just as we celebrate Independence Day on July 4 in commemoration of the signing of the Declaration of Independence in Philadelphia, June 19 is Freedom Day. It celebrates Abraham Lincoln's Emancipation Proclamation.

But the Emancipation Proclamation was signed on January 1, 1863. Juneteenth commemorates the news that the slaves were free reaching Galveston, Texas, two and a half years later. Legend tells of a messenger bearing the news of the executive order being murdered on his way. Another version suggests that the news was deliberately withheld so that an extra crop could be gathered in.

Yet another story points out that Texas was unimpressed by the Union President's wartime authority over that area and didn't honor the order until sufficient military was present to force them. By June 19th, 1865, the freeing of slaves had been written into the Constitution as the 13th amendment. It would be signed by the requisite number of states within a few months. General Lee had surrendered the Confederacy and the reunited US military had authority to enforce Constitutional law.

So, Juneteenth 2015 was the 150th anniversary. The beaches of Galveston were sprinkled with sunbathers and children playing in the surf. The aroma of barbecue was thick in the air. As we strolled toward a beach side amusement park, our (very blonde) grandkids spotted a playground.

The park was crowded with little black children and their parents. Everyone seemed happy and excited and we soon struck up conversations with the adults. The lady I chatted with was there with her grandkids. She seemed surprised that I knew about Juneteenth. "There's going to be a parade come by here in an hour or so and then they'll have fireworks over the pier," she explained. "You should stay."

But it was dinnertime. We hadn't thought to pack a picnic and our bellies overruled our brains. If we waited, the parade would close the road for several hours. It seemed like too much to ask our little ones.

But we celebrated Freedom Day with ice cream sundaes and family fellowship. We explained it to the children as well as we could.

Though Juneteenth is honored mostly by Black Americans, all those who love liberty and justice can rejoice in the blessings of freedom.

The 13th amendment didn't solve all race relations. It didn't fully establish justice and mercy and opportunity for all. The so-called 'Jim Crow' laws, prohibiting public race integration and equal rights continued until **July 1964** when President Lyndon Johnson signed the Civil Rights Act. Black Americans were not even given the right to vote until **1965**!

Author George Santayana is quoted as saying, "Those who do not learn history are doomed to repeat it." It seems to me that if that is true, Slavery will take on a different form, wear a different costume and masquerade as civil rights.

But the USA is making progress. I plan to celebrate Juneteenth every year now. I'm going to make sure that my grandkids know where America has been so that they can lengthen our national stride in making this a land of liberty and justice for all. I hope that they will always be comfortable with a playground filled with others of another race.

Only in America, God Bless it.

Chapter 18

Buffalo Make a Stand in Custer State Park

George Armstrong Custer wheedled his way into West Point. After being disciplined several times and nearly expelled, he finished dead last in his class. But the Civil war was starting and the Union was desperate enough for officers to take him.

Custer distinguished himself in several important battles, miraculously surviving many dangerous maneuvers. Though he consistently reported high casualties in his divisions, he was quickly advanced in rank. His reputation as a reckless and brutal man deepened as he fought the Lakota Sioux and Southern Cheyenne Indians.

But one expedition before his demise at Little Bighorn eventually gave him a 71,000-acre park named after him. He had been sent to find a good location in the Black Hills for a fort. When his expedition found gold too, his reports caused a gold rush in the Black Hills.

Custer is best remembered by his demise at Little Bighorn in what is now Montana. But Custer State Park in South Dakota offers camping and fishing and loads of wildlife. I'd always wanted to see a wild buffalo.

A free-ranging herd of about 1,450 buffalo, (American Bison) roams the park uninhibited. When our family visited there, we pressed our noses to the window glass, hoping to see one. How we cheered when we spotted one, with his furry backside just disappearing over a distant rise. Whew! We were lucky to look that way just in time!

We went another few miles and came upon *another* buffalo standing right in the middle of the road. This one-ton beast eyed our puny minivan with malevolence in his bloodshot eyes. We deemed it wise to await his pleasure to move from the road, or not, rather than annoy him with a car horn.

He was just a crossing guard. Within a few seconds, buffalo started pouring over a steep ridge above us, charging down the incline, engulfing our minivan in an avalanche of gigantic, furry bodies. They're so front-end heavy that they threaten to stumble head over heels with every step. It would only take one of those monsters hitting our car to topple us into the Ravine of Oblivion on the opposite side of the car.

One of the littler kids started to whimper. My mouth was about the only thing that was dry, and I tend to keep silent when I'm scared spitless. At least 'trampled by buffalo would make an interesting obituary.

But they swerved around us like we were nothing more than a boulder, forgetting us before their scent in our nostrils had faded.

A little further along the highway, we pulled over so I could retrieve some buffalo fur from a tree where one had rubbed. It's extremely soft, almost like long baby hair, with little odor.

Though George Custer named the area 'Custer Park' himself, the parallel of natives thundering over a ridge, our lives forfeit to their mood, certainly brought "last stand" to my mind.

It's a vast, beautiful, wild country. I don't think the buffalo, pronghorns, deer and elk much care what name it bears. Call it what you want, it's a place worth knowing.

Only in America, God Bless it.

Buffalo at Custer State Park, South Dakota

Chapter 19

When in Philadelphia, Order Cheesesteak

Apple pie, baseball and credit card debt move over. What could be more quintessential American than Philly Cheesesteak?

I suppose I'd had one here or there before my first trip to Philadelphia, but never knew they were controversial, nor did I know about the distinct ordering protocol.

Legend says that a street hotdog vendor named Pat Olivieri one day tossed steak on his grill and the aroma attracted cabbies like bees to honeysuckle. Before long, he opened Pat's King of Steaks to sell his new creation. Eventually, he claims, he had the idea to add cheese to the recipe.

Joe Vento, who opened Geno's across the street from Pat's, claims that it was *he* that added the cheese and so *his* is truly the original cheesesteak sandwich.

A Philly Cheesesteak sandwich is sautéed ribeye steak, sliced or chopped and stuffed inside a crusty roll. Cheese Whiz, (probably not really cheese at all) is the common accompaniment, with provolone or American acceptable substitutes.

Nobody likes to look like an uninformed clod, so here's all you need to know to seem like a native. You need only three words. If you're ordering one sandwich with cheese whiz and the traditional grilled onions, you just say, 'one whiz with'. If you say 'one American without' you'll get one sandwich with American cheese and no onions.

 When my son was in dental school in Philly, 'Chubby's Whiz with' won his fervent loyalty. My son is anything but chubby, which is not to be said of the proprietor.

Oh, yes, indeed it was a fine, flavorful meal. Beefy and juicy and the roll had plenty of body to stand up to the moisture of the meat and onions. When I first saw the bulging wrappers, I thought I'd never be able to eat the whole thing in one sitting. I intended to divide the gastronomical delight into two meals. Didn't happen. I just couldn't stop eating. I blamed it on Chubby.

Knowing that the competition over Philly Cheesesteaks is fierce, I ordered another one when we visited the historic Reading Terminal Market. You know the one from the movie National Treasure where she hides behind the meat counter? I have concluded that it's hard to go far wrong ordering Philly Cheesesteak in Philadelphia. In fact, even away from there, if it has "Philly" in the name, you're probably in for something lovely. Taste of Philly Sub Shop in Crystal River, Florida is anecdotal proof of my name-equals-deliciousness theory. Piles of succulent beef perky with onions and melded with cheese had us rhapsodizing all afternoon.

Wanting to preempt anemia before a diagnosis, I recently needed a philly cheesesteak for medicinal purposes . I ordered one in Packards in downtown Oklahoma City. The presentation was suspect, with green peppers sautéed with the onions. The waitress didn't even ask me "Whiz with?"

Maybe it had been awhile since I had my previous Cheesesteak. But it was a day trip to the land of gastro delights. Vibrant flavors balanced between beef and cheese, enthroned perfectly on a generous crusty roll. Packards has earned the right to add 'Philly' to their signage.

Only in America, God Bless it!

Of course, other than cheesesteak, another main Philadelphia attraction is the Liberty Bell (seen here with Independence Hall in the background)

Chapter 20

America's Giants

There are trees you can drive through in Northern California. They're tourist hotspots when the beaches are socked in with fog, so they get a lot of traffic.

 The thrill of it is not actually driving through the giant redwood, but rather having someone else drive through it and taking a picture of your car coming through the one-car-garage-sized opening.

Though the practice of cutting tunnels in single trees started over 100 years ago, it doesn't kill them. They hardly seem to notice. They're tough old giants.

Tannins in their wood make them resistant to insects, fire and rot. My parents once owned a piece of property covered with the old trees in Central California in Santa Cruz County. When my Dad decided to build a deck on a 15 foot diameter stump, the wood was still sound. It had been cut at least 50 years earlier.

New trees spring up all around a stump. Dad milled two of the younger trees that had sprouted in the ring around his deck stump for use in the exposed beams and woodwork of the house.

 They can grow 100 feet in 50 years and reach heights of over 300 feet. Some of the trees thriving along the coast of California today were already towering through the fog when the cross of Jesus was cut and fashioned.

Now Giant Sequoias grow nowhere else but the cool, foggy coast of central and northern California and southern Oregon.

But there are giant redwoods in Colorado, too. The Florissant Fossil Beds, about 30 miles west of Colorado Springs, displays many giant stumps of petrified redwoods. Abundant fossils of their leaves and cones lie entombed in the shale around them.

The area was once the site of a major volcanic eruption. A vast super-hot mudflow buried the giants' roots in mud and collected so much debris that it dammed a valley that subsequently filled with water. Water and volcanic mud are two super heroes for turning wood to stone.

Their presence there implies that the conditions in Colorado were once vastly different than now. At 8,000 feet, fog is rare and the air is thin.

There are two other species in the region of the petrified redwoods in Colorado that are each older even than California's redwoods and giant sequoias. Aspens grow in multi-trunk clones, sharing roots between the whole grove. Aspen clones are thought to be not only the oldest living organism on earth, but also the heaviest.

Bristlecone pines also live in the Rockies and parts of the Sierra Nevada Mountains. They are the oldest individual trees living. Some of the ugly, twisted specimens alive today were alive when Abraham found a ram in a thicket on Mt. Moriah.

But for all the records they don't hold, coastal redwoods are certainly the tallest living organisms on earth, and their first cousins, the giant sequoias are the largest by volume. They both soar into the gray, coastal skies, their tops vanishing in the swirling mists. If the day is warm, it's always cool in the deep green shade of the giant redwoods.

Doesn't it just make you want to cut a tunnel though one so you can drive through it?

Only in America, God Bless it.

Beth Stephenson

Chapter 21

NORAD is the Stuff of Movies

Cheyenne Mountain near Colorado Springs is almost a foothill of Pikes Peak. An acronym for North American Aerospace Defense Command, it is a joint effort with Canada for monitoring and defending the skies over the US and its nearest northern neighbor. The purpose of the facility is to monitor everything that flies or threatens to fly into US and Canadian airspace. NORAD knows about every missile test, every pass of a satellite and every bit of space junk that orbits the earth. Even model rocket launches over a certain size can show up as a blip on the super-sensitive monitors. It's the stuff of farfetched action movies, and almost unbelievable in its complexity.

NORAD was built inside a man-made cave in Cheyenne Mountain. Gigantic doors designed to withstand tremendous assault from a variety of powerful weapons admit workers to a mile-long tunnel into the midnight cavern. 15 two and three story buildings ride on gigantic springs to protect them from explosions or earthquakes. All plumbing flexes, too.

When the cavern inside Cheyenne Mountain was being excavated in the early sixties, an artesian well sprung up, almost causing the engineer to scrap that site. Instead, they created a 1.5 million gallon reservoir for the cold, clear water and it continues to supply the facility with more water than it needs. The boats for maintaining sit motionless as though waiting for passengers on the River Styx.

I visited NORAD with a troop of Boy Scouts before the facility was closed to tours after 9/11/2001. Even then, we were thoroughly screened before receiving clearance to glimpse some of our nations' defense facilities.

Our guide showed us a room through a glass wall where a huge electronic map was displayed. The guide calmly explained the acute sensitivity of the devices, and a few "what ifs." As we watched bright spots develop and fade on the screen, a subtle alarm sounded. Curtains closed automatically, obscuring our view. We were whisked entirely out of the building for a scintillating description of the mountain's water system. We asked what might have caused our sudden expulsion, but the guide politely refused to explain.

The site is called "hardened" because of the natural defenses as well as the elaborate preparations against attack. It is impervious to an electromagnetic pulse and non-government entities contract space there for that reason. The bunker is built to deflect a 30 megaton nuclear explosion from within about a mile. There are 25-ton blast doors in side tunnels that can be opened by multiple methods. The facility is also equipped with multiple layers of unique filters to capture air-borne contaminants.

 NORAD has redundant power sources, and can be encapsulated for extended periods without danger and little discomfort for those sheltered inside. They keep cots and food on hand, just in case. The joint commanders of the facility report directly to the President of the United States and the Canadian Prime Minister. The American is always a four star general or equivalent, with headquarters at Peterson Air Force Base, and the Canadian is always a three star general.

 I'm glad for the diligence of those monitoring our safety.

Only in (North) America, God bless it.

Beth Stephenson

Chapter 22

Mountain Monograms

In the western part of the United States, whole communities succumb to the urge to display their school or community pride by stamping their initial on the sides of mountains. Some are painted on stone and some are overlaid with painted concrete or rocks and some are created by strategically clearcutting dense vegetation. Whatever the method, there are over 500 mountain monograms in the US, mostly west of the Great Plains.

Since cave people began doodling away the cold winter months by writing on cave walls, the market for washable wall paint had its roots. Every parent has had to deal with childish graphic indiscretions. But communities protect their civic geoglyphs with law and taxes. Students defend their mountainside symbols from desecration from rivals with the ardor of a band of campaigning knights.

The first mountain monogram was created in 1905 by UC Berkeley students. The seventy-foot-high yellow 'C' was widely protested when first conceived. Opponents claimed it would be 'vulgar' and "for all time disfigure the sensuous beauty of the hills." But building the 'C' successfully diffused the out of hand 'rush week' hazing between the Freshmen and Sophomore classes. Cal permanently changed its tradition to painting the hillside 'C' yellow.

Vulgar or not, the Cal monogram created a fashion craze. Shortly after its appearance, the University of Utah's freshmen and sophomores united to paint a 100 foot-high U on a hillside overlooking the campus in Salt Lake City.

Not to be outdone by their rivals, the following year Brigham Young University students undertook to paint 'BYU' on a mountain just south of campus. It was an ideal site, with an accessible surface with room for all three letters. But after a grueling 6-hour paint bucket brigade, they had only finished the 380-foot high 'Y'. The largest in existence at the time, it was deemed good enough. Now both the University of Utah and Brigham Young University are commonly referred to by their monograms, the 'U' and the 'Y.'

As children, mountain monograms diverted our attention on the dead boring drive between Grandma's house in Salt Lake City and our home on the coast of California. Battle Mountain, NV has both its initials drawn on the mountain. The inevitable comment about seeing "a B.M. on the mountain" always drew a laugh in our entertainment-starved state.

Now, all the Wasatch mountain front needs is for Linden, UT to get an 'L. Geographically it is between Pleasant Grove, which has an impressive 'G' and BYU with their 'Y'. The 'U' is in the north. That way, flying south from the Salt Lake International Airport, the mountain range would read U.G.L.Y. It isn't true, but it would be something for Wikipedia to note.

The monograms become rallying points for civic or school spirit. They are often lit for special occasions, repainted as part of homecoming celebrations and targeted by rival schools. In BYU legend, the story is told of the night the Utah Utes undertook to bloody BYU's Y under a coat of red paint. When they got to the gigantic block letter, they realized they had vastly underestimated its size. The splashes of red paint they tossed on top of the fresh whitewash merely gave it a mild case of the measles.

I am uncertain whether mountain monograms are protected by the First Amendment. But communities that sport them, love them.

Only in America, God Bless it.

Beth Stephenson

Chapter 23

Arch Endures as Towering Symbol of Spirit

We were moving 2,000 miles to the east. On the third day, I was farther east than I'd ever been in my 15 years of life.

Heat and humidity intensified. I could hardly wait to get to our new home to get out of the humidity.

At last we arrived in St. Louis, Missouri and the tiny house my dad had rented. After a week of living on expense-account restaurant food, we feasted on weenies and beans and cranked up the air conditioning. I'd never lived in a house with air conditioning. I gawked at the neighbors that sat outside at night in matching 98 degree heat and humidity.

Within a few days, we visited the Icon of St. Louis. The Gateway Arch soared over the old Riverfront downtown, its stainless steel skin sparkling in the brilliant sun. We had traveled 2,000 miles east, only to find the Gateway to the West.

The arch had only been finished for about a decade. The locals were unabashedly proud of it. Their first question to us newcomers was "Have you seen the Arch?" They each seemed eager to explain its origins and elements.

I gazed up at the sloping triangular towers meeting impossibly high overhead and wondered what it meant. Why an arch? What was it *good* for?

It had been conceived in 1933 as the Jefferson National Expansion Memorial Association (JNEMA—pronounced "Jenny May") Officially, it's a monument to Thomas Jefferson, for his westward looking national vision, and all the pioneers, settlers and explorers who braved the unknown to settle the western frontier.

At the height of the Great Depression, there were many who had the same thought I had. Monuments are great on a full stomach, but many hungry Americans and Missourians wanted a more practical project.

But it was promoted as a way to rejuvenate the Riverfront area of St. Louis, invite tourism, provide employment, and encourage investment. The best part was that St. Louis would end up with a towering symbol of the American spirt.

But a world war was fought and the USA had to climb into a period of consistent prosperity before the project gained any real traction. Architect Eero Saarinen won the design competition in 1948. After 17 more years of delays, having undergone union walkouts, accusations that the arch was a symbol of tyranny (Romans?) aesthetic battles and underfunding, it was finished.

However impractical, it didn't take long for me to fall in love with my Arch. Soaring 630 feet above the earth and sunk 60 feet into concrete and bedrock, it's visible all over the city. It's mathematical perfection and grace speaks boldly of American ideas and ideals. A trip in a tram car to the top brings visitors into a triangular room with the walls sloping outward. It's a strange sensation to lean almost on your tummy and appreciate the sweeping view 63 stories below. It's sort of like architectural hang gliding.

Each year, the Gateway Arch has about 4 million people visit the surrounding park and museum with about a million buying tram tickets for a ride to the top.

The Gateway to the West turned 50 last year. An arch, structurally strong, built on deep rock foundations, a shining symbol of what it means to be American.

Only in America, God bless it.

Chapter 24

Ever Tasted Squirrel?

I was new to Oklahoma and still enthralled by all the fruit trees and nut trees that garden catalogs claimed would thrive. I'd sat on my back porch, reading the catalog hyperbole about pecan trees while watching half a dozen squirrels raid my bird feeder. A few weeks later, I met an elderly native Oklahoman and asked her if she had any experience growing pecans.

"Well of course. We'd gather a gunny sack full and sit out on the porch to crack them."

"How'd you keep the squirrels from stealing them all?"

She looked at me like I was stupid. "We'd shoot 'em!"

"With what?"

"My dad had a little rifle for squirrels. He'd put me on his back and we'd go out in the afternoon and watch for them." She studied me thoughtfully for a moment. "People don't eat squirrel much anymore, do they?"

"I guess not. What does it taste like?"

"Squirrel."

I didn't press her.

The subject came up again recently with a friend who is a Juilliard School of Music graduate. Mercedes Rousseau grew up in Indiana and even in her mid-nineties can not only play any tune she hears, but add elaborate embellishments. She's bent and twig thin, but sparkles with energy. Once you get Mercedes talking, she always has a story ready.

"Once, a soldier gave me an envelope hat and a book on military tactics. I loved to put on my hat and go out with my rifle and imagine what tactics I would use.

"We had sixty acres of woods and my mother had a problem with squirrels in the attic. The pest control people couldn't do anything about it, and when the pest man came to check, he stepped through our ceiling and dumped insulation all over the floor. He wished he hadn't gotten out of bed that day and we did, too.

"So I told my mothe r that I'd get rid of the squirrels from the attic. I filled the bird feeder and got my gun and opened the window.

When the squirrels came to the bird feeder, I'd shoot from the open window. I killed thirty squirrels with that single shot rifle before they stopped getting into our attic.

"Course we'd eat 'em and I decided to tan the hides. I used salt and alum. You can use hydrochloric acid, but that's dangerous stuff and the salt and alum worked fine."

"What did you do with all the squirrel hides? I asked.

"It wasn't just squirrels, I'd get some rabbits and once I got a raccoon. I don't think we ate the raccoon, but we ate the rabbits before I tanned the hides. I traded all of them for violin lessons."

"What were they worth in money, back then?"

"I have no idea. I never thought of converting them to money when the violin teacher took them as payment."

She summed up the conversation. "When you want or need something, you figure out a way to get what you want. I sold hides." She shook her finger at me. "That's what we do in this country. When you know what you want, you have to go after it. Find a way."

Words to live by.

Only in America, God Bless it!

Chapter 25

Fair Sailing or Fare Sale-ing

In the midst of WW1, my grandparents were married. My little grandma was a lovely little woman with a 19 inch waist, blue eyes and dark brown hair. Though she had been raised in aristocratic society, money was tight. So she and her mother did exactly what we do today when we want nicer stuff but don't want to pay the price. They went garage sale-ing.

Grandmother told the tale when she gave me the dresser she had bought before she died. She and her mother wisely started in the nicest part of town where a house offered lots of furniture. "I loved the graceful dresser and chest of drawers set, but I only had enough money for one of them. They were solid walnut." She bought the dresser with its oval mirror and feminine lines with the hope that she could earn enough money in time to come back for the chest. She never got it.

I had cherished the dresser in my own home for fifteen years when a friend called me to come take a look at the score she had made at a garage sale. She had tried a new splatter paint method over a solid color paint and was jazzed by the result.

My heart sank in my chest as I studied the cheerful project. Same lines, same detail. "Is it walnut?"

"Yes, it was really dark, but it's well made and I love the detail."

"If you ever decide to sell that piece, call me first."

She grinned. "I don't think I'm going to be selling it."In garage sale-ing, the race is to the swift.

 "It's just that it's the matching piece to an antique dresser my grandmother gave me." I told her the story. She didn't even bother to contrive the proper look of sympathy.

I've had my own big scores. Two years ago I found a handmade Turkish rug, a pair of chest waders for my fisherman son that FIT him perfectly, and the exact table for my living room I'd been wanting for months, all for a total of $33. That evening, another son came to visit and he and his wife hurried over and bought a 5 piece, solid wood bedroom set for $200 and an electronic piano.

The down side of garage sales is that if you get it home and it isn't right, there are no returns. I once bought 5 wet suits for $10 each.

When I proudly displayed them to my husband, he asked the obvious. "Where do you plan to use them?"

Garage Sale-ing has become both a pastime and profession. Treasure hunters scour sales for bargains to keep or resell. I have a friend that likes to know what her friends are looking for and to go out hunting for the best bargain she can find for them. She found a nearly new riding mower for me for less than half price.

Lots of my friends claim garage sale-ing as a hobby. I streamlined my treasure hunting by joining a Facebook group where I can shop and sell without spending much time or fuel.

I still keep a lookout for another mate to Grandmother's old dresser. But perhaps the fishing waders and the living room table will be heirlooms to my own grandchildren someday.

Only in America, God bless it!

Grandmother bought this dresser at a yard sale in 1918

Chapter 26

Tourists Fall for Niagra Falls

I walked to Canada and spent that night in Mexico when I was seven months pregnant with our seventh child. Before the DHS officials get all hot and bothered, let me explain.

We had an almost-new Ford club wagon that seated 12. There were only 8 ½ of us on the trip. After my brother's wedding in Chicago, we were on our way to Niagara Falls and points beyond.

People drive hundreds of miles to see water falling off a cliff. But the liquid roars like a perpetual storm, splashing an eternal mist onto the faces of awestruck tourists. It's power rumbles in your core and shrivels your ego to ant-size. Humans like to be humbled now and then.

The thought of walking across on a tightrope as Jean-Francios

Gravelet did first in 1859 was enough to induce morning sickness in a man.

Of the twelve people that have launched themselves over the brink, the first was a woman, proving gender equality in the insanity department. Some have used barrels, a jet ski or other homemade contraptions. A few have survived to pay the stiff fine. One who did survive was banned from ever reentering Canada. Another survived a swim over Niagara Falls in nothing but swimming trunks, but his drunk friend couldn't operate the video camera and it wasn't recorded.

It seems strange that nobody turns off the water at night. Even when nobody's watching, 30 million gallons of water on average plunge over the crest of The Falls each minute. It would take 22 minutes for Niagara Falls to supply the State of Arizona with its total daily water usage.

Nearly three quarters of the water in the Niagara River is diverted upstream to run a mammoth hydro-electric plant in New York. The water is returned to the river downstream of The Falls, so a full volume Niagara Falls, (not seen for over a century) requires a powerful imagination. This is where the walking to Canada part comes in. The border was established in 1819 and no amount of arguing had convinced the Canadians to give up most of Horseshoe Falls.

Niagara Falls are actually three separate falls on the Niagara River. The American Falls and Bridal Veil Falls are entirely in the US. But the largest of the three is Horseshoe Falls and it is partly in Canada. The only really good view of it requires a jaunt across the bridge into Canada.

Even pregnant, I wanted to brag that I had walked (waddled) to Canada. Nowadays, you need a passport for adults and a copy of a birth certificate for minors.

It was a hot day and the route to the best Canadian observation point was farther than it looked. But I did it. We have the photos to prove it.

By the time we packed ourselves back into the van, we were tired and hungry. We had a reservation at a KOA camp in Mexico, New York. It was dark and raining by the time we got there. The rest of the family slept in a soggy tent but I slept well that night in Mexico on the back seat of the van.

Only in America, God Bless it.

Four of my sons at Niagra Falls

Chapter 27

Wild Bears Bear Watching

The haze lay low in the canyons and the ridges faded in shades of blue in the distance. I was replete with a sense of peace. Gone was the anxiousness I sometimes feel as a tourist. I've seen what I wanted to see.

Topping my list was a real live bear. Not the caged kind that I've seen in zoos that are hardly more active than a rug. I wanted to see a genuine papa bear that might eat Goldilocks for stepping into his hillbilly house in the Great Smoky Mountains.

Jeff and I love waterfalls and there were dozens of breathtaking scenes to explore in that national park. The park spans the state line between Tennessee and North Carolina, and was made a national park in 1934.

I think it was our fourth day and about our sixth waterfall. Sweat already stung my eyes with less than a mile behind us and about that far to go. The bear warning signs seemed intended to impress gullible tourists.

Ferns and mosses jeweled the banks of chuckling streams along the trail with quiet wildflowers peeking out from virginal forest nooks. The smell of the sun on the pines and wet verdure and fallen leaves accented the joyful songs of colorful birds. Butterflies and dragon flies lilted on the fitful breeze. The SD card in my new auto-focus-auto exposure camera was bursting with prissy snowdrops and ferny dells.

Here and there, we glimpsed vultures circling wide around the region, like Satan looking for an entrance to the Garden of Eden. Jeff carried a lightweight aspen walking stick worn smooth from use. Gnarled roots entwined rocks on the trail and we placed our feet with care. It wouldn't do to sprain an ankle.

Some early bird hikers approached from the direction of the waterfall. "Watch out for the bear. He's a pretty good size."

A bear! Those were the glorious words I'd longed to hear.

"Just up the trail, maybe fifty yards."

Just then, a humongous black bear appeared about thirty feet away.

My camera dangled forgotten at the sight of that giant Ursus Americanus.

Oh, my, what big teeth he had! Not that I could actually see them, but I knew they were there. He surveyed us as he nibbled some delicacy, edging closer. We were frozen with something like excitement but more similar to panic. I suddenly realized that zoos have a reason to put a wide moat or thick glass between those who wish to gaze on living bears.

The bear had seen a tourist or two and apparently wasn't in the mood for a few salty, red-faced gawkers. He lumbered on down the slope, barely blinking his beady eyes in our direction.

It took ten minutes for Jeff to ask if anyone got a picture. He might have gotten the same answer if he'd asked if anyone had dry pants.

It was the next day when the sense of peace and delight settled on me. I'd seen a black bear in the wild of the Great Smoky Mountains. I even lived to tell about it.

Only in Amcrica, God Bless it.

We saw this bear later on the trip in Cade's Cove, Smoky Mountain National Park. Fortunately, this one wasn't so close & we had time to get the camera out!

Beth Stephenson

Chapter 28

American Pie Might be French Pastry in St. Genevieve, MO

There is a sweet little Missouri town just an hour south of St. Louis on the Mississippi River named St. Genevieve. In the summer, the verdant hills are seamed with creeks and patches of hardwood trees. The rich alluvial soil that attracted early settlers, still sustains a network of farms and wineries. By mid-July, the corn is as high as an elephant's eye. At the nearby Cave Winery, 15 acres of grapes yields an average of 50 tons of grapes and each ton produces 160 gallons of juice.

Tourists wander the quiet streets of St. Genevieve, stepping in and out of deliberately quaint antique stores and museums. First built by French from Canada and the Caribbean Islands long before Thomas Jefferson made the Louisiana Purchase, the French influence has not been buried either by other ethnic influences or the power of Old Man River.

Just to the south of the town center, several national historic places are notable for their rarity. Perhaps the French folks in 1755 were feeling perverse, or perhaps they didn't know any better, but they chose to build their houses tipped sideways.

Instead of laying logs sideways and notching the corners to hold it together like any self-respecting Anglo Saxon, they planted the posts in the earth pointing skyward, filled in the spaces with rocks and lime mortar, and then plastered the walls with more lime-based stucco.

Aside from being proof that there was no building code in those days, the local French Colonial style buildings probably survived water and termites because of readily available limestone. Lime is naturally unfriendly to termites and wood-rotting fungus.

The historic sites each boast the typical French construction, with wide, covered porches and balconies and hipped roofs. St. Genevieve is especially interesting because of the extreme rarity of the post-in-the-earth-style houses surviving to tell the tale. Some are furnished with the belongings of the wealthy families who lived there. Some gained their wealth by trading furs they bought from Native Americans.

La Maison de Guibourd on 4th and Merchant still has original slave quarters. I enjoyed seeing the Norman French trusses in the attic, too.

By 1830, an influx of immigrants from the Black Forest

area of Germany fled a poor economy and political unrest to come to St. Genevieve for a piece of the American pie. They built tall, plain, brick homes with lots of function and little grace. Yet they have little trouble outwitting vermin and I wonder if the original settlers noticed a similar contrast.

But the little village is notable for more than its early history. In 1993, the mighty Mississippi got drunk on spring rains and raged through hundreds of communities that lay on his banks. St. Genevieve took warning early and began sandbagging and reinforcing their levy.

Resident Mickey Koetting tells of history-loving strangers coming to help. She remembers townspeople and restaurants working day and night to sustain sandbaggers and those operating heavy equipment to reinforce the dyke. "People heard what was going on and came to help." St. Genevieve mostly dodged the destruction that year when over a thousand US counties were disaster areas.

John Audubon of 19th century bird fame lived and did business in town. I ate at his namesake restaurant and it was fantastic. I'm not much of a shopper, but even I was impressed by the great prices in the antique shops. I paid just $8 for a charming Christmas tree ornament in the ASL Pewter Foundry. Craftsman Thomas Hooper was spinning metal plates into a base for pitchers to fill an order from Williamsburg, VA. He took a break to demonstrate the use of sealing a letter with a wax seal for us.

French and Germans, Native Americans and Africans built St. Genevieve. It's a delightful little melting pot.

Only in America, God Bless it.

Mickey Koetting points out the French architecture at a historic home in St. Genevieve, MO

Chapter 29

Historically All-Black Towns are Unique US Treasures

I had never heard of a black town until I met Andre and Jessilyn Head. What a strange concept it was to me at first: towns across America, built for blacks, by blacks. I could hardly believe it at first. As 21st Century Americans, don't we strive to consider men and women based not on the color of their skin but the content of their character?

But black towns predate the dream that Martin Luther King iterated. Most of them sprang up in the fifty years following the Civil war.

The first post-emancipation town was called Nicodemus. I assume the name has reference to Jesus telling the Pharisee named Nicodemus that man must be born again of the spirit. The town Nicodemus was to be a new birth, a place on the Kansas frontier where newly freed slaves could prosper without persecution.

The soil in Nicodemus was asserted to be so wonderfully rich that it yielded abundant crops with very little effort. Advertising called it the Promised Land where there would be no houses of "ill repute" or saloons for the first five years at least. The cost to go to Nicodemus was five dollars, to be paid if necessary in installments.

But when hopeful settlers arrived at the infant community, they found people living in dugouts and conditions very different from the florid advertising.

Even with disappointments, the idea of building safe, self-sustaining communities continued to attract black citizens. Nicodemus eventually thrived and encouraged as many as 200 black communities across the country, though many were not incorporated.

I met Andre and Jessilyn Head at a seminar titled 'Black Towns Then and Now' at the Oklahoma History Center. I heard of strong communities building happy, healthy towns. I saw old photos of proud business owners and thriving commerce.

The first building erected was invariably a church, often doubling as a school. Businesses and homes sprang up around that central edifice, both symbolically and geographically. No doubt each village had its share of scoundrels and heroes, workers and bums.

But history indicates that they were generally industrious and eager to give their children a better future.

The most astonishing thing I learned that night was that a handful of these 'black towns,' still exist and maintain a distinct black identity. In the age of information and high tech gadgetry, low-tech towns struggle with modern realities, regardless of their history. Opportunities for youth are as limited in a small black hometown as they are in any small town.

Boley Oklahoma was once (and perhaps is still) the richest of all of the black towns. Each summer since 1903, the Boley Rodeo and BBQ Festival attracts droves of visitors. That transfusion of money keeps lifeblood flowing.

The town of Langston, OK was built as a black town. But the Langston University student body is only 84% African American with almost double the number of females to males. Even with the University, the town faces many small-town dilemmas.

The Heads have high hopes for some of the other surviving black towns in Oklahoma, too. They visit with town leaders to develop methods for creating an inflow of money and solving the common civic problems. Through the Coltrane Group, they organize Black Town Tours each spring and fall for tourists to learn the history and experience the warm, welcoming culture of a few of the living towns.

Whether the towns will die out as residents age remains to be seen. But the all-black towns of this country remind me how far we've come and that there is still work to be done. They are historical treasures and uniquely American.

Only in America, God bless it.

An image from the historically all-black town of Nicodemus, KS [Library of Congress]

Chapter 30

When Dreams of being an American Olympian Come True

Lopez Lomong clutched the American flag with two hands as he led the American Olympic team into the opening ceremonies in Beijing. He is a black man, born in South Sudan and brought to America, as he explains in his autobiography *Running for my Life*, "by the grace and power of God".

His mother named him 'Lopepe' which means 'fast.' He loved to run and he loved to work. He was constantly at his parents' elbows, asking for tasks, wanting to help.

One Sunday when he was six years old, trucks full of rebel soldiers surrounded an outdoor church service. With all the children in church that day, Little Lopepe was torn from his mother's arms and taken to a training camp. The girls were separated from the boys and never seen again. Boys either turned into soldiers or died.

He'd gotten used to seeing dead boys each morning when three older boys helped him escape with them. They thought they were going home, but ended up in a Kenyan refugee camp with tens of thousands of other lost boys.

Lopepe told himself his parents couldn't rescue him because they were dead. The highlight of each week was when the trucks brought the garbage into the camp for the boys to scavenge through. The U.N. brought in monthly rations. On Christmas and Easter, his family of ten tentmates made soup with the whole chicken they received.

The camp school operated using sticks to scratch lessons in the dirt. There were no books. Only the luckiest sponsored boys had paper and pencils. The teacher hit him if he made a mistake.

A wad of rags substituted as a soccer ball. The older boys said that nobody played until they ran a 30 kilometer lap around the camp. Running set him free by taking his mind off of his empty belly and his hopeless existence.

A farmer paid him fifty cents for work on a farm, but his friends pressured him into spending it to watch something called "The

Olympics" on the same farmer's grainy TV.

Michael Johnson won a gold medal. Lopepe (now Lopez) had never known that some Americans were black or that running was a sport. Johnson ran with his head up, back straight, so fast, so strong. To be American must be the pinnacle of joy. Lopez began to dream.

Then one Sunday the camp minister announced that 3,500 boys were going to be taken to foster homes in America. All they had to do was write an essay. . .in English.

It was a miracle. Lopez wrote his personal history. He loved to work and he loved 'football'. He wanted to go to America because he wanted to work to help his friends. His campmates helped him translate from Swahili into English. Lopez knew it was a miracle from God when his name was read. He would not waste it.

His foster parents told him to call them 'Mom' and 'Dad.' They gave him a whole chicken sandwich. At first he took cold showers because he didn't know there was hot water in the pipe. He didn't know how to turn the light off. Using the indoor bathroom seemed disrespectful of his fabulous new home.

Speaking little English and with a second grade level education, his foster mom insisted he was to graduate with his class. She helped him night and day.

The high school cross country coach bribed him into joining the team by offering him a jacket with his name on the back. He easily won meets. What was five kilometers when he was used to running thirty every day?

"It was God's miracle" he says, that he graduated with his age group. He went on to college. He realized his dream of becoming an American citizen, and qualified for the Olympics. In 2008, his fellow Olympians elected him to bear the American flag in the opening ceremonies.

He calls meeting President George W. Bush and Laura Bush his highest honor. The President had heard his story and chatted with him before the 2008 Games. "Lopez, be careful not to let the flag touch the ground."

A lost boy from the killing fields of Sudan, who survived 10 years in a Kenyan refugee camp, wears the American flag on his jersey in Track and Field again in 2016. He earned a college degree. The Lopez Lomong (www.LopezLomong.com) charitable foundation helps bring clean water, education and modern farming techniques to South Sudan.

He has not wasted the chance he received by the grace of God.

Only in America, God bless it.

RUNNING
FOR MY LIFE

One Lost Boy's Journey from the Killing Fields of Sudan to the Olympic Games

U.S. Olympic Athlete

LOPEZ LOMONG

with Mark Tabb

Beth Stephenson

Chapter 31

A True American Lady

My heart beat faster. My throat constricted. There she was: her face set in resolution. Her arm was raised, holding a beacon: a torch, an invitation as well as a guiding, welcoming light. The flame of the torch is freedom.

Jeff's nerves were frayed from driving our new twelve passenger van through the streets of Manhattan. He thrust the map into my hands, asking me to navigate. But I could hardly take my eyes off of her.

My eyes welled up so that I couldn't read the map and before we knew it, we were re-crossing the Harbor.

Jeff managed to get the van pointed back into Manhattan Island. When at last the valet had parked our behemoth vehicle we packed into a ferry. Until that day, I thought the Statue of Liberty was on Ellis Island. It made sense Ellis Island was an immigrant's first footfall on American soil. There, they were checked to verify that they carried no disease and that their legal papers were in order. Some were turned back but for those granted entrance, their names and personal data were recorded. The spelling of their names was often left to the best guess of the recorder, especially if they spoke little English. Some of those misspellings have carried over into present days.

Finally, they travelled that last tiny span of water to the Land of the Free and the Home of the Brave.

I quickly understood that Lady Liberty has her own island. It's hard to imagine how gigantic she is until you're standing at her feet. She's 151 feet tall and a little more than double that with the pedestal. Her nose is four and a half feet long!

She was Frenchman Edouard de Laboulaye's brainchild. She was to be a gift to the United States to commemorate her Centennial birthday. Ten years later, sculptor Frederic Auguste Bartholdi got the commission to build her. The US was responsible for the pedestal and the French would take care of the statue and her assembly in the US. They raised the money with fundraisers like bake sales on both sides of the sea.

Her true name is "Liberty Enlightening the World.' The sonnet in her pedestal is named "The New Colossus" referencing the Colossus of Rhodes which legend suggests stood at the harbor mouth on the Island of Rhodes in Greece. But that Colossus was built to Helios, the Greek sun god, to commemorate a military victory.

Lady Liberty stands for an idea, not a political statement. She faces the harbor mouth like a hostess stands beside the door of her home, welcoming freedom–loving newcomers and homecomers alike.

I planted myself in front of the plaque inside the pedestal and stood still while tourists jostled all around me. Tears gathered in my eyes and ran down my cheeks. It didn't matter. I wish everyone from sea to shining sea could read and remember the message Emma Lazarus penned on behalf of this nation.

The New Colossus

Not like the brazen giant of Greek fame,
With conquering limbs astride from land to land;
Here at our sea-washed, sunset gates shall stand
A mighty woman with a torch, whose flame
Is the imprisoned lightning, and her name
Mother of Exiles. From her beacon-hand
Glows world-wide welcome; her mild eyes command
The air-bridged harbor that twin cities frame.
"Keep ancient lands, your storied pomp!" cries she
With silent lips. "Give me your tired, your poor,
Your huddled masses yearning to breathe free,
The wretched refuse of your teeming shore.
Send these, the homeless, tempest-tost to me,
I lift my lamp beside the golden door!"

Only in America, God bless it!

Standing on top of the pedestal looking up at Lady Liberty

Chapter 32

Alaska Shows it's Wild and Wooly Side

I could hardly close my eyes as the twilight continued on toward morning. It was summer in Alaska, and though we were visiting Denali National Park well past the summer solstice, there was plenty of midnight sun to go around the clock. I'd been up until two in the morning the week before photographing the sun almost setting behind some jagged peaks. It never quite got the job done. But once we got to Denali, we were farther north and the farthest east we would travel on that trip. Earlier in the day, we'd gone for a hike in the boulder-strewn scrubby growth. There was none of the dense, wet vegetation we'd seen earlier in Juneau and Ketchikan. Cold blue-green rivers rushed toward the sea, with occasional elk and deer stopping to drink.

We'd been in the area for two days already, and though the namesake mountain is 20,237 feet high, it had not shed its veil of mist. It would be three more days before we finally glimpsed the peak of the highest mountain in North America. Even in summer, it's capped with perpetual ice and snow.

We couldn't even figure out what to call it. In grade school, I learned that Mt. McKinley is the highest mountain in the country. But Alaskans weren't satisfied with the name, given by a gold prospector in honor of the US President William McKinley. They favored the local tribal name, Denali, meaning 'the high one.' But when they petitioned congress to change the name of the mountain, (national parks fall under the federal government), an Ohio senator blocked the change. It seems Ohio is William McKinley's birthplace.

The USA bought Alaska from the Russians for just over seven million dollars immediately after the end of the Civil War. It was nicknamed 'Seward's Folly' after Secretary of State William Seward. People started to rethink the nickname when gold was discovered. World War 2 proved its strategic importance. It became the 49th state in 1959.

Our son Brian and his wife Kelsi spent two summers in Juneau as bus tour guides. They took us to a gold mine that had been abandoned with much of the machinery left in the woods to rust away. Gold mines still operate in many parts of the state.

The Juneau region has all the flora and fauna of a typical rain forest plus bears, salmon and bald eagles. We took a tour of hanging gardens where trees have been stood on their trunks with their roots in the air and the flowers planted on top. They

apparently get plenty of water, since it rains nearly every day in the
summer.

**In Juneau we found a stream where the salmon were so
numerous Thomas pulled them out by hand**

The salmon were running and our kids took us to a stream where
the fish are just turning in from the sea. A fish gate keeps
undesirable varieties of salmon from overwhelming the more
valuable types, although I have no idea how the gate sorts out the
losers. The thing that struck me most about Alaska is the vast
wildness of it. While there are a few thriving towns, mostly along

the west coast, the rugged mountains seem to go on forever. Glaciers grind canyons, calving into the sea or lakes day and night.

Fishermen stand almost shoulder to shoulder, pulling out huge salmon on the Kenai River while Grizzly bears fish just a few hundred feet downstream.

The people we met seemed fiercely independent and self-sufficient. They were kind to us tourists, but I had the sense that if I wanted to fit in, I'd have to prove my mettle. It's not a place for wimps.

Only in America, God Bless it.

Big tires for rough terrain. Thomas, Me, Jeff and Tricia

Chapter 33

Backpacking in Targhee National Forest

We stepped off the trail to let the ranger pass. He was on horseback, with a lean, wiry build and skin tanned dark as his saddle. He grinned at us. What a job!

My backpack was not as heavy as it looked. I'd put the sleeping bag and pad inside and carried a few clothes and camp necessities. Carrying gear in a pack effectively weeds out the luxuries. My son Chris had volunteered to carry some of the extra weight. Besides that, the slowest person determines the pace and it was an easy guess that which one of us that would be. Jeff had his Indiana Jones hat, (crushable and waterproof) and his Rascal Beater walking stick. He carried more weight than I did and soon discovered that his pack was not as comfortable as mine, either.

We were on the Upper Palisades Lake trail in the Targhee National Forest in Idaho. Though it was mid-August, the leaves on some of the flora were donning their autumn colors. Since it was a weekday, we had the trail mostly to ourselves and the lakes entirely to ourselves. The afternoon was comfortably warm and the creek tumbled snowmelt as though summer was just beginning.

I guess the rugged cliffs and steep scree fields above us were cut by glaciers long ago. The stony outcroppings and overlooks are ideal for mountain lions. One of the hikers coming down the trail said they saw a bear near there the day before. Another hiker told us to watch for moose at Lower Palisades Lake.

The sound of the rushing creek and the smell of the sun on the willows combined with the beautiful scenery awakens a yearning in me, almost to sadness. My meager camera can't capture the spell of the place. I try to notice everything: to plant the memory deep for safekeeping.

We set up camp in a primitive campground, with the only improvement being a three-sided outhouse. We boiled water for our delicious dehydrated meals. Two fawns wandered into camp, galloping away if we moved too suddenly then tiptoeing meekly back.

A few minutes after Chris left to wash the dishes, we heard him yelling for us to come to the lake. Two moose were grazing on the lake moss. They posed long enough for some good pictures but we moved off when they got closer. Jeff had a bull moose saunter right past him the next morning and later Chris and I also saw the big fellow grazing in the willows.

It's a fairly level hike with a bit of an uphill push just below the lower lake. We camped at the lower lake and hiked to the upper without our packs the next day. The trail between the lakes is a bit more rugged with steeper sections. The stream itself is mostly slower, with occasional beaver ponds. Fishermen nodded or murmured a greeting, but quickly returned to their silent sport. Chicken Springs gushes out of the mountain just when we began to yearn for a cold drink.

I imagine Paradise will look something like Upper Palisades Lake. We slaked our thirst with the crystal, cold aquamarine-colored water. I listened to the insects humming in the wildflowers while I soaked my feet. I hoped the minnows around the shore would give me a pedicure, but they contented themselves with lingering in the shade of my legs. We watched trout tease Chris's fishing lures with no intention of biting. He finally gave up on the fish. He dove in and came up shouting at the cold.

I have cataloged another spectacular place in one of our National Forests. You and I own a little bit of that place.

Only in America, God bless it.

The moose was busy chomping on grasses in the lake while Chris cleaned our dishes

Chapter 34

Remembering Dad

There's a nip in the evening air and the first leaves are donning their costumes for the third act of the yearly play. Pumpkins and Halloween costumes have begun to appear in the stores and apples are blushing in the cold.

It all adds up to one thing: football!

I grew up in a football household. My dad, Hal Mitchell, was an all-star at UCLA and went on to play a season as a tackle for the New York Giants. When he was hurt in spring practice and cut from the team, he was immediately drafted into the army.

He told the story of showing up at Ft. Lee, Virginia.

He gave his name. The receiving officer asked him, "Are you THE Hal Mitchell, the football player?"

"Yep."

"Report to the fieldhouse." In those days, each branch of the military had their own team. They were not quite pro, but more like semi-pro. "I can't play football. I have a knee injury."The officer apparently looked him over. "Lieutenant, either report to the fieldhouse or go to Korea. It's up to you."

He was captain of the Army football team. But Dad was a creative man with the mind of an engineer. He designed a knee brace/pad that would protect his particular injury. The knee healed, even through the rigors of football. He went on to design a whole pad system that protected players better with a better range of motion in the shoulders. He patented the pad system and eventually sold it to Rawlings Sporting Goods. He spent the last decade of his employment years as head of research and development for Rawlings.

Dad turned to coaching after the army because he didn't want the life of a professional football player for his growing family. He was offered a 5-year no-cut guarantee contract with the Washington Redskins but he turned them down. He became an assistant coach at Saugus High School and taught math and P.E.

After a few years, BYU solicited his application as the freshman coach.

Many years later, I visited the fieldhouse at BYU. I didn't remember much about Dad's old stomping grounds, but the smell of sweat and disinfectant and leather called up the friendly ghosts of my early childhood.

Dad's BYU freshman team had been undefeated for two years when he was given the head coaching job. BYU is owned by The Church of Jesus Christ of Latter-day Saints and has a strict honor code. Recognizing the major disadvantage in recruiting, Dad philosophized that the best recruiting tool was winning games. He'd played the single wing offense under Red Sanders at UCLA and thought that running that out-of-fashion offense would give BYU the edge they needed, since opponents would be less familiar with it.

The only coach in the region using the single wing was a high school coach named LaVell Edwards, so he hired him as an assistant.

Dad was the Western Athletic Conference Coach of the Year in his second year of coaching the Varsity. But the single wing was marked for death and most of their opponents apparently managed to defend it pretty handily. They didn't win much.

At the very beginning of his third year, he kicked a few starters off the team for honor code violations. That was the beginning of the end of his career at BYU. The president of the university pressured him to reinstate the players. Earnest Wilkinson was running for public office and resented the bad publicity the team had attracted. Under threat of firing from Wilkinson dad replied, "You can force me to reinstate them, but you can't make me play them." They sat on the bench the entire season. I remember him coming home from work looking very pale. He hung his fedora on a hook and said, "I've been fired." All kinds of terrible images crossed my four-year-old mind.

In the years that followed, each of those five players contacted him to tell him that his courage in sticking with the moral principle that cost him his job had been a turning point for good in their lives. They had each straightened up and thrived.

He spent the next 11 years coaching at Cabrillo College on the Monterey Bay in California. He left Cabrillo to work in R&D for Rawlings.

But the fall in our family is scheduled around the football schedule.

Tis the season for tailgating and cheering yourself hoarse. Football optimism abounds.

Only in America, God bless it!

Hal Mitchell at UCLA in 1951

Chapter 35

Morgantown Tomato Fairy

Nobody really strolls the residential areas of Morgantown, West Virginia. It's not that the streets aren't charming and it's not that there's nothing to see. It's not even that the weather doesn't permit it. It's in the semantics of the word 'stroll'. "To walk at a leisurely pace," implies casual effort and that's where the difficulty arises. If you're enjoying the architectural variety or gardens of the Morgantown neighborhoods, particularly South Park, you're better off in hiking boots than walking shoes.

Not to say that it isn't worth it. Our son Daniel and his family have lived in Morgantown for three years and with each visit, we enjoy exploring the neighborhoods built into the steep slopes. Morgantown is home to the University of West Virginia Mountaineers. What the name lacks in creativity, it makes up for in accuracy.

Historic Building designations are a dime a dozen, from the grand to the quaint. Deep front porches with gabled second stories seem to have been popular in the last two centuries. Victorian mansions stand side by side with craftsmen cottages.

It was one such cottage that caught my attention for the vegetable garden that rioted in the tiny front yard. Tomato plants craned their necks above a vining squash that invaded every available nook. Peppers had turned leggy in their quest for sunlight, and drying dill blossoms crowned the whole scene with abundant seed heads.

"Look at this garden gone crazy!" I exclaimed. "Tomatoes and squash and peppers! The squash is trying to take over the world!"

"Did you read the sign?" I had not noticed that the owner was sitting on her porch. I hadn't read the message on the front of her porch rail, either, since most of the lettering was obscured by the vines. It said something like 'This garden is for sharing, for your senses and ours."

She introduced herself as Eve. Like the Bishop of Digne in Les Miserables, she had created a thief-proof garden!

The middle-aged gardener reiterated the invitation. "You're welcome to whatever you want whenever you want to come pick. I especially enjoy sharing with children."

My 3-year-old granddaughter Kate's eyes lit up as she leapt out of her stroller. "I want to pick something!" My son explained that they had planted some vegetables in the back yard of their apartment complex, but it hadn't yielded much. (It's too shady for anything to produce well).

Eve led Kate to the most accessible tomato plant and found the prettiest, unblemished tomatoes. Once Kate had a few stowed in her stroller tray, she noticed the cherry tomatoes hanging like clusters of red grapes. When she had all her little hands could manage, she told the benefactress thank you.

"Come back for more whenever you want."

I couldn't resist taking a dill seed head. I had scattered the old seed at the home we just sold and it hadn't been ready to harvest when we moved. Eve laughed when I asked for it. "I said you can take what you want. But what are you going to use it for?" she said.

"I'm going to scatter the seed in the spring. I love to grow my own cucumbers, dill and garlic and make pickles."

Her eyes lit up. "Oh really! Well, good luck."

I have a feeling that next year might see cucumbers added to her garden and pickles added to the menus of her neighbors.

Only in America, God bless it.

Lettering on the rail explains the Sharing Garden

Chapter 36

The Legacy of the Glider Pilots

Another September 11th has passed and I am musing on the sacrifices of those Americans called upon to defend freedom and human rights in the world.

My uncle Harold flew a fighter plane in the Pacific theater and my husband's grandfather, Delbert (Bus) Bingham flew a glider into Market Garden, Holland in World War II.

On a recent visit to the Silent Wings Museum in Lubbock, TX , I learned a bit more about gliders and their pilots.

A plane with no engine makes no noise and is invisible on radar. A glider is nothing more than a frame with treated canvas stretched over it. Its maximum load was thirteen soldiers or even a jeep with five soldiers plus a pilot and copilot. The tow plane would haul the glider near the front lines, drop the tow rope and the glider pilot would guide the plane to a predetermined site where they would more or less crash land. There were skids on the front of the craft so that they would ski along the ground without flipping.

Almost before they halted, they'd have the nose of the plane up and the cargo dispatched.

It goes without saying that such a voyage was incredibly dangerous. When gliders were first used in Sicily, 139 gliders went in, but when there was heavy fire from the ground, the tow planes dropped the lines too early and only 49 of the gliders made it to shore. It nearly cost the army the glider program.

Most of the American glider pilots were trained in Lubbock, TX. A genuine WW2 glider reposes in the Silent Wings Museum there. As I stroked the flimsy canvas skin, surveyed wooden benches where the troops sat and gazed into the back of the cockpit, Grandpa Bingham's stories came to life.

He told of being stationed in North Africa, waiting to be sent into battle. The men he had trained with in Lubbock had become his dear friends. Then one night after about two weeks of waiting, his squad was called up to be ready to leave before dawn the next day. But Bus woke with flu-like symptoms. He assured the commander that it would pass, but he was running a high fever and was commanded back to bed. His friends and comrades flew the mission without him. None of them returned.

It was the battle of Market Garden in Holland when Bus finally got to test his wings. He described the exhilaration as the glider was pulled into the sky. As they approached the target, a bullet from the ground pierced the canvas between the copilot's feet, struck the copilot through the chin and straight up into his brain. He was killed instantly. Bus flew on. There was no turning back in a plane without an engine. He found the target landing spot but until they had landed, they did not know that the enemy lines had shifted several miles during the night and Bus and his cargo of soldiers were in enemy territory.

They could hear the battle going on ahead of them. They hid during the day and zig-zagged their way to friendlier turf.

Back in Ogden, UT, his loved ones and sweetheart read his name on the list of Missing in Action.

Grandpa didn't often tell his war stories. When his progeny asked questions about the war, he'd answer briefly. Only in his last years did he elaborate with more details. He realized that young Americans, who have never known want or war needed to know the price of freedom. The pilots, along with uncounted others, offered their lives on the altar of human rights in the cause of human liberty and justice.

I wandered through a multitude of exhibits in the city where the glider pilots once learned the knack of crashing with grace. Silver wing pins with a 'G' in the middle identified the Gliders. Some say the 'G' stood for 'guts.'

Now, Grandpa Bingham, like most of the 6,000 WW2 glider pilots have made their last flight into heaven. But may the legacy of those freedom lovers never die.

Only in America, God Bless it.

The nose of the glider opened up for the jeep to roll out.

IN MEMORY OF ALL WORLD WAR II GLIDER
PILOTS WHO RECEIVED ADVANCE TRAINING
AND SILVER 'G' WINGS AT SOUTH PLAINS
ARMY AIR FIELD, LUBBOCK TEXAS DURING
THE PERIOD OF 13 JULY 1942
THROUGH 15 JANUARY 1945.

THESE VOLUNTEERS FLEW FRAGILE, UNARMED
GLIDERS ON EIGHT MAJOR AIRBORNE INVASIONS
OF EUROPE AND SOUTHEAST ASIA. MANY PAID
THE SUPREME SACRIFICE FOR THEIR COUNTRY.

PRESENTED TO THE CITY OF LUBBOCK
BY

THE NATIONAL WW II GLIDER PILOTS ASSOCIATION
"WE FEW, WE HAPPY FEW, WE BAND OF BROTHERS"
19 APRIL 1997

WACO, 15-MAN, GLIDER (CG-4A)

Chapter 37

Rescue Workers are Knights in Shining Armor

I was just trying to catch some air. I'd been watching my 7-year-old grandson sail over the jumps at the bike park we were visiting. My son urged me to go a little faster on my new mountain bike to "catch some air."

It was certain to make an awesome photograph, so I handed my son my camera and decided that when I reached the peak of the berm, I wouldn't brake, as instinct suggested, but I would let myself launch into the clear, blue air. I didn't realize that when he instructed me to stand up on the pedals as I went over the jump he meant that it was necessary to the physics of the stunt. Standing up seemed a little too daring.

My front tire hugged the trail like a Bridgestone and the back tire behaved more like a hang glider. My body most resembled a sky diver without a chute.

I remember the sensation of my helmet grinding in the gravel as the rest of my body tumbled over. Oh I hurt. I wasn't sure I wasn't broken to bits, but as I tried this limb and then another, I seemed mostly in one bleeding piece. I gingerly rose from the dust and allowed my husband and son to guide me down the trail. I became more and more disoriented as I walked toward the car. I didn't know where I was or where I lived. I knew that I must have some level of brain injury, and told my husband to call 911. He says I said it at least half a dozen times.

My husband tells me that the sheriff arrived within a minute and helped reassure all involved. I don't remember that part.

The next thing I remember is a paramedic talking to me. He was asking me questions and narrating what he was doing as he took my blood pressure and did a preliminary assessment.

I don't remember actually seeing his face. I have the impression that he was a young, handsome, fellow but that impression is probably based mostly on my preconceived ideas of knights in shining armor and rescue workers.

Maybe I've been incredibly lucky in the rescue workers that have responded to my urgent calls, but I don't think it's luck. Experience suggests that all rescue workers are calm, sympathetic, knowledgeable, friendly and capable.

I've seen police at accident scenes calming and reassuring those involved in the incident with tremendous compassion, particularly those who were at fault and knew it.

Another time, a young guest fell unconscious on our living room floor and when he came around, showed symptoms of having a heart attack. Rescue workers were there in a few moments and correctly identified the source of his distress (panic and hyperventilation) so that by the time the ambulance arrived, he was already feeling pretty good.

The time my son Brian filleted his fingers in the midst of a Colorado blizzard, it took the volunteer fire department rescue workers half an hour to get through the deep snow to our house. But the dispatcher on the 911 line calmly instructed me what to do and what was likely to happen. When the EMT's did arrive, they calmly surveyed the ghastly injury as they joked with my son. By the time they climbed out of the ambulance at the hospital, they were laughing and joking like fast friends.

Another time, I tore my hamstring water skiing. If given a choice between that or childbirth, I'd take childbirth twice. I was so grateful that my brother-in-law, Barry Baxter, is an EMT and fireman. He not only knew exactly how to best convey me into the boat, his calm confidence reassured me and helped me to be calm enough to assess my own injury.

Rescue workers' calm, controlled presence is enough to stop someone from going into shock. I haven't figured out whether only people with the attributes of calm, confidence, and competence think of going into those fields or whether that reassuring demeanor is the result of terrific training.

I'm healing up pretty quickly from my career as a stunt cyclist. The brain scan showed no damage. Unfortunately, my son looked away at just the wrong moment and didn't get a picture.

But I'm feeling grateful for those that I know are standing by to come to our rescue. Thank you to all the thousands of men and women who minister to us in our most frightening moments. Every time you help someone, you claim a lifelong tender spot in someone's heart.

Only in America, God bless it!

My son Rob demonstrates how to catch air on a jump. This photo was taken just moments before I crashed while attempting such a jump

Chapter 38

Shakin' it Up

My Mom wanted a tart. I'm not talking about the sassy girl type of tart, I mean a butter crust, jam filled hand tart. Raspberry to be exact. "If you go to a Shakespeare play," she insisted, "you have to have a tart." We weren't sure they were still offered so late in the season.

I guess I'd never heard about the Shakespeare tart rule. But we had just watched *Julius Caesar* at the Utah Shakespearean Festival in Cedar City and were about to find our seats for Neil Simon's *The Odd Couple.* Shakespearean festivals in America have morphed into a mix of classic American dramas mixed with the Bard.

Apparently, we weren't the only ones intent on procuring tarts. A middle-aged man pressed his palms and forehead against the retractable wall under a sign which read "REFRESHMENTS". There were a number of folks already in line ahead of us, too.

I ordered 'summer berry.' A sticky filling peeked demurely from the folds of a tender, sweet, butter crust. Oh my! No wonder Shakespearean festivals are as common in the USA as in England!

With a degree in English and American Literature, I'm obligated to love Shakespeare. My husband Jeff's degree is in accounting and he feels no such duty. He shamelessly buys tickets to traveling Broadway musicals. In fact, he sat out in the warm Utah afternoon reading a Clive Cussler novel while we curdled our hearts over Julius Caesar's ancient assassination. Well, to each his own. Or should I say, 'As You Like It'?

All 50 states and even some of the US territories produce Shakespeare plays each year. The Utah Shakespeare Festival on the Southern Utah University Campus in Cedar City boasts two replica versions of the Globe Theater where The Bard's plays were first performed. During the summer, there's also a free green show where magicians, jugglers, and other circus-type acts entertain between short theatrical scenes on the rolling lawns.

 Even the National Foundation of the Arts has a special grant specifically for Shakespearean productions. You'd almost think Old Willy was an American, with so Much Ado.

I have a theory that Americans are drawn to Shakespeare by the same impulse that makes family history research so popular. With the Bible and Homer's Odyssey, Shakespeare is one of the patriarchs of not only American literature but much of our culture, too.

But American Anglophilia can lead to a comedy of errors. Three summers ago, I bought season tickets to Shakespeare in the Park in OKC. Most of the plays were performed in the charming outdoor theater in Myriad Gardens. The audience is separated from the stage by nothing more than a narrow moat and actors enter and exit via bridges that lead through the aisles of the audience.

Our daughter, Tricia was newly married to a loveable, innocent guy, Walt, who had seen more off-roading trails than dramatic presentations. He'd never been to a Shakespeare play. I was eager to impress him with our exalted culture and well-rounded interests. I invited the newlyweds to accompany us to the opening performance of Measure for Measure. A comedy seemed guaranteed to entertain and delight. We sat near the front on stage left. Scene one opened with The Duke in western clothing, sitting a few feet in front of us. Enter a Marilyn Monroe look alike who stepped up onto his desk. He loosened his necktie and unbuttoned his shirt as he watched her unclothe on his desk.

I started to sweat, not knowing how far Fair Marilyn would go. Jeff shot me a meaningful scowl. How was I supposed to know?

Thankfully, the scene was interrupted when it got to the PG-13 stage. But I was tense for the rest of play, worried that they'd take further embarrassing license. I must say, Ol' William definitely had a bawdy sense of humor. It isn't as noticeable until you hear and see it acted out on stage.

Walt and Tricia thanked us graciously for the "treat," but I don't think either have been to a Shakespeare play since.

William Shakespeare may not have been American, but in our great melting pot of cultures, he's an important seasoning in our American stew. Soon, cities all across the nation will unveil next summer's menus of Shakespeare offerings. If you take a taste, you'll learn a little of what roots grew us into the story, laughter and hero-loving nation we are.

Only in America, God Bless it.

A new theatre on the Southern Utah University campus in Cedar City is reminiscent of London's Globe.

Chapter 39

Rock Climbing in Yosemite

I think if I had known that the name Yosemite means "those who kill" in the Native American tongue of Miwok, I would have declined an invitation to go rock climbing there. Add to that, the friends who invited me were the Hazards. Sometimes you don't have to be a mountain man or an Indian guide to read the trail signs.

But then again, Yosemite boasts some of the most spectacular scenery in the world. I simply couldn't resist the outing, nor the opportunity to brag that I'd been rock climbing in Yosemite.

The name was not meant to refer to the soaring cliffs and roaring waterfalls, but rather to the band of renegade outcasts, particularly from Paiute tribes, who lived there. The Miwoks and the Paiutes were traditional enemies. L.H. Bunnell of the Mariposa Battalion named the valley, but he thought the Native word meant 'grizzly bear.' The mistake stemmed from using too much sign language as the natives tried to convey that the looming cliffs encircle the valley like the jaws of a bear.

He claimed he chose the name because the astonishing scenery defied description with any European language. He decided to use the native American word for a uniquely American place.

I suppose that regardless of the accuracy of the name, the most powerful tribes got first choice of where to live. There's a reason they chose Yosemite Valley. Not only is there plenty of game, (an old fashioned word for 'wildlife,') the icy, clear Merced River rushes through the valley. There's plenty of timber and other than the valley mouth, there isn't much possibility for a surprise attack.

I've been to Yosemite many times. It's often crowded with visitors snapping pictures. Laughing streams gurgle like happy infants until they pitch over deathly precipices. One of the fish native to Yosemite has the practical name of 'hardhead.' I suppose those floating upside down are called 'Not-Hard-Enough-Head.'

The most famous sites in Yosemite are El Capitan and Half Dome. The day we went to climb, the famous precipices were dotted with climbers like flecks of pepper on a vertical snow field.

Climbing partners take turns belaying each other up level after level. Expert rock climbers on multiday climbs link hammocks to the rock faces for a peaceful night dangling a thousand feet above a valley floor.

Rappelling is not a social condition, but the word for harnessing up

with ropes and walking down a cliff backward. Once you're over the initial lip of the cliff and it's too late to go back, it's great fun. I'd been rappelling in college.

Experienced rock climbers know that only expert climbers attempt something as daunting as Half Dome. Not even our host was qualified at that level.

Fortunately, there are lots of mini-cliffs on the giant boulders left like a comet's tail from vanished glaciers.

Greg Hazard picked out a likely spot for us beginners. It was a little away from the teeming tourists. From the top of the rock, you could see the Merced river falling all over itself on its way to the sea. The warm sun charmed the vanilla scent from the Ponderosa Pines. Half Dome and El Capitan itched with the human fleas on their faces.

I climbed up the steep back of the rock without ropes. But fifteen feet above terra firma seems a lot higher from the top. Self preservation instinct demanded that I reconsider. But we'd come a long way and I didn't want my friends to think I was ungrateful.

I backed off the edge, feeling the rope take my weight. I pushed off the rock with my feet, letting a little rope slide through my fingers to control the speed of my descent.

Half Dome (Photo by Lynda Baxter)

Within a few seconds, my sneakers met the California soil. I could truthfully brag that I'd been rock climbing in Yosemite. I think I'll have it printed on a tee shirt.

Only in America, God bless it.

Chapter 40

Of Cats and Dogs

I left my front door open because the delivery men needed to make several trips. A neighbor's opportunist cat decided that would be a good time to check out the inside of our house.

She's a black and white short-haired little creature that purred the instant I picked her up. I pretend not to know that she's taken to napping on our front porch furniture.

I admit that I'm tempted to offer her a little treat. If I wanted a cat, she'd be a nice one.

But I don't want a cat. I'm quite satisfied to enjoy the neighbor's pets occasionally and then leave them to their masters.

The American Pets Products Association estimates that there are roughly even numbers of cats and dogs in the USA, but the number of households with dogs is higher than the number with cats. Apparently cat people are more likely to have multiple cats.

Pets are big business. Almost 80 million American households have a pet. In the last 5 years, the number of household with pets has gone up more than 20%, though the percentage with multiple pets has diminished by about the same percentage. Apparently, about 13 million families have relatively new pets, but most of those new pet owners didn't get multiple animals.

During that same time, the amount of money spent on vet bills per pet multiplied by eight.

I recently stopped over at my Mom's house to check on her cat while she was out of town. Molly is a long-haired, black and white shedding machine. Molly mostly sulks under Mom's bed when left alone. She greets me with a 'mew' but comes out from under the bed only if I pop the lid on a can of cat food or rustle the dry food in her bowl.

That day, I treated Molly to some canned food and left her to eat it. I left the back door open while I went out back to help Jeff pick the last of Mom's raspberries. That way, Molly could survey her kingdom from the back steps once she was finished with her delicate repast.

A little later, the next-door neighbor dog, Bruno, loped over to lick

our hands. He's a glossy Irish Setter who takes all kinds of liberties with friendly neighbors. I petted him a bit while he slapped my legs with his feathery tail. His owner soon came to claim him with the traditional apology. "He's no problem," I said. "He's a nice pup."

I went back into the house to put the raspberries in Mom's freezer and lock up when I noticed that every lick of the cat food was gone. Even the overkill pan of extra food and water stood empty. Molly can't eat three cups of dry food in 15 minutes.

Bruno.

I told on him to my mom. Apparently it wasn't the first time he'd sponged up Molly's food.

But neighbor dogs and cats are like neighborhood children. They're fun to have around, as long as they don't do anything ugly in my yard, and even if they are greedy beasts.

I once heard a sheriff give a talk on Women's safety. He commented that there are many ways to protect oneself from evil people, but in his opinion, the best deterrent was a dog. He believed that it didn't make much difference whether it's a big dog or a little one. "Anything that barks." He must have been a dog guy.

Cats make nice lap warmers. If you have a mouse problem a cat with intact claws will solve it, right after it scratches the stuffing out of your living room sofa.

So today, I put the patchy kitty out of my house three times before the delivery men had finished. She blinked demurely as she curled up on the patio chair on my front porch. An unreasoning pleasure tickled my lips. It's nice to be popular.

Only in America, God Bless it.

The neighbor's cat reclines on our patio chair

Chapter 41
The Florida Keys

I had always associated the Florida Keys with an exotic hangout of the rich and famous. So when we lumbered over the bridge to Key Largo in our ancient RV, our faces peered out of every window. Like most things of legend, the reality was not what I had imagined.

The Keys are a 127 mile long chain of small coral islands that run from the southeastern tip of Florida to Key West. We call them 'Keys' as an adaptation of the Spanish word, 'Cayo' meaning 'small island'. They were formed in ancient times when the world was much warmer and the entire southern half of Florida was under a shallow sea. Reefs built the structures of the region. When an ice age slurped up vast quantities of ocean water into the polar caps, the oceans dropped as much as 300 to 350 feet below its current level. They refilled as the ice age ended and the shorelines for the low-lying keys have remained about the same since Ponce

Son Brian also found a nice shell, but it also had an occupant!

De Leon first discovered them in the 1500's.

The first thing that surprised me was that there are hundreds of islands! Some of them are not big enough for a cat to live on comfortably. They dot the path of the chain of bridges like freckles on a redhead.

You would think with so many tropical islands, beaches would be a dime a dozen. There are beaches, but the majority of them are man-made with imported sand. Not true, however of Bahia Honda State Park. The island has the lovely distinction of not needing man to supplement Mother Nature's idea of an ideal coral island.

We had reserved a parking spot for the RV and backed into our slot with the back bumper about 10 feet from the Gulf. Within a minute, some of our kids had donned swim suits and snorkeling gear while others were breaking out the fishing gear.

There are tent camping sites, but with the humidity, bugs and heat, summer camping would ruin the experience. Prices for rentals, restaurants, lodging and attractions are lower in the summer for the same reasons.

Key West is decked out to be a tourist attraction all year, with a nightly Sunset Celebration. While the sunset was pretty spectacular, the jugglers, magicians, artists, food vendors and musicians at Mallory Square were equally intriguing.

The warm Florida sea teems with tropical fish, conches, (pronounced konks). We enjoyed watching the lobsters in the marina, too. The vast stretches of white sand beach on the other side of the island have sea turtle nests roped off with 'do not disturb' signs pinned on them. Raccoons keep a close watch on careless picnickers. Mosquitoes feast.

There's a commercial area in the park where tourists can rent sea kayaks by the hour. On a different trip, sans the RV and kids, Jeff and I rented a double kayak and paddled out to a nearby island that is part of the Bahia Honda Wildlife area. We took turns diving in about 8 feet of water while the other kept the kayak nearby. We pulled up huge conches, but they all still had living residents, so we returned them to the ocean floor. Snorkeling tours show tropical reefs and shallow fields of sea grass.

Ernest Hemingway spent some of the last years of his life in Key West and visitors can tour his home.

The Florida Keys are a tropical destination without the wallet shock that comes with other destinations.

Only in America, God Bless it.

Look what I found! Kayaking near Bahia Honda, Florida Keys. Unfortunately, the living conch was still in the shell, so I didn't keep it.

Beth Stephenson

Chapter 42

Origins of Halloween

Halloween didn't start in America. Like most of the holidays deeply ingrained in our culture, its roots stem from our non-American ancestors. Here's a handful of facts.

The Celts were the first to celebrate the end of October with a holiday called Samhain (pronounced So-in). They believed that summer ended on October 31 and the long uncertain winter began. Summer and harvest were associated with life and winter and darkness with death. They also believed that the line between the mortal world and the immortal world was blurred on that night. They dressed in costumes to disguise themselves from roaming ghosts, ghouls and demons. Witches were suspected of turning themselves into black cats. Fortune telling, especially young maids attempting to identify their future husbands, abounded. Anything that brought bad luck, (spilling salt, walking under a ladder, etc.) was a bad omen for the beginning of the season of death.

The Roman Empire conquered the Celtic lands that are now Ireland. As the Roman empire became Christianized, so their conquered lands followed. But the popes were uneasy with the residual Celtic superstitions and created a substitute holiday on November 1. All Saints day was a day to remember the Saints and martyrs. People were urged to dress as saints and angels.

Parties became the celebration of choice and celebrations attracted beggars. They promised to pray for the souls of dead ancestors in exchange for food or money. The activity of soliciting Hallowed Eve gifts was once called "going a-souling."

In the early colonization days of America, the heavily Protestant churches strongly discouraged anything either Catholic or Pagan. Other than in renegade Maryland and some other southern areas, it wasn't until the potato famine in Ireland in the 1840's that multitudes of displaced Irish brought their mixed Celt-Catholic traditions and the date of October 31 began to get some attention.

For the most part, the American iteration of the date removed religious overtones and kept the party element. The eve of the hallowed or holy day when saints were to be honored became Hallowed Eve, then Hallowe'en and finally Halloween.

Modern Trick or Treating seems to be an American concept started during the Great Depression. Then, as now, a giant bowl of candy was insurance against marauding ghouls of diminutive years or stature. Just as schools make multitudes of rules governing costumes, even at its inception, local governments discouraged costumes that were gruesome or scary. Late in the 20th Century, the candy making companies perpetuated a fraud when they began making miniature candy bars and named them 'fun-sized.'

When I was of trick or treating age, (alas, the time has passed), we still dressed as tramps, witches, ghosts and angels with boys often choosing to be football players or cowboys. Storybook characters were also common. The luckiest girls got to be fairies.

As I raised my children, I made traditional Halloween costumes out of polyester so they would last for generations. My kids longed for disposable superhero capes and glamorous garbage.

Now, thousands of kiddos extort goodies from their neighbors on Halloween. Each year, an average of six billion dollars are spent, and one quarter of the candy purchased in the US each year is purchased as bribes to little beggars.

Movie superheroes, Harry Potter characters and Disney Princesses scurry from house to house like a sudden infestation of rats. Dentists rejoice that next year's income is once again assured.

I'm well-stocked with minuscule candy bars and the pumpkins are carved to glare down anyone who doesn't appreciate my sense of fun.

Only in America, God bless it.

World War II Veteran Jack G Clark
Photo sent by his son Jack "Chip" Clark.

Chapter 43

A Veteran's Story

For much of my life, I have lived near cities with Air Force bases and Army posts.

Members of the military are naturally as diverse as the general population except in one aspect that seems uniformly true. They are patriotic, freedom-loving people who see America as worth fighting and sacrificing for.

A recent *Americana* column about the WW2 Glider Pilots inspired some readers to tell me the stories of their family heroes. All of them were touching in their courage and sacrifices. Here are some excerpts from one first-hand account shared by Jack G Clark with his family who in turn shared it with me.

"Dear Family,

On this date 60 years ago, the 440th Troop Carrier of the 9th Air Force had all of its serviceable C47s lined up, two by two, on the runway at A10, our airbase just outside Orleans, France. An equal number of CG12A Waco gliders were on the grass bordering the runway-half on one side, half on the other. Each glider was connected by a long bungee cord to the plane that was going to tow it to the LZ (landing zone) in Germany, some miles beyond the Rhine River."

After describing the formation and the mission, he continues:

"The pilots of the 440th who were posted to fly that day had been awakened early and treated to a fine breakfast of steak and eggs- real eggs! You can't imagine how good real eggs taste unless you've been eating powdered eggs for months. Then we all piled into the 6x6 trucks for a ride out to A10.

The gliders were already loaded with high explosives and airborne engineers. Their job, once we arrived at the LZ was to blow up bridges and fortifications.

After a while the first c47s began to take off, each pulling a CG13A. Before long it was our turn. Our group was due at the LZ at noon, and as I remember, it was about a 2 hour flight. But it takes a long time to get all those aircraft in the air and into the necessary formation. My glider was #2 in an echelon of 4 to the right Churning along toward the Rhine the formation was a bit loose, but as we got close to the river, the tow planes and hence the gliders pulled in tight.

Our briefing had indicated the Rhine would be a beehive of activity with Allied assault boats ferrying British troops across to fight their way inland to our LZ. However, when we arrived at the river and I looked down, it was completely devoid of activity. Looking ahead to the far shore, I saw a solid gray curtain of flak and gun smoke. That flak and smoke was constant all the rest of the way in to the LZ.

Approach altitude was 1200 feet and once you got a green light from the tow plane and cut loose, you were supposed to turn (in formation of course) 270 degrees to the left. I was gliding on number one in my echelon, who was ahead and on my left, and also glancing at #3 who was behind on my right. Once when I looked back at #3 there was nothing but a big black puff of smoke. He had taken a direct hit and the explosives on board had detonated. It was about then I noticed in my wing about six inches outboard from my head, a big hole where a German 88 shell had gone through. Those 88s were fused to explode on contact, but evidently the one that went through my wing was a dud."

Mr. Clark describes the Landing Zone as littered with crashed gliders because they were all overloaded. The engineers on his plane jumped out while it was still moving 50-60 miles per hour to avoid being shot by the enemy as they exited the plane. He unhooked his harness and ran to ditch where there was a little protection.

For the next few days, they functioned as infantrymen, guarding POW's. He continues.

"The night before the mission, one of my good friends, Lt. Burmeister, was disconsolate because he had not been posted to fly the next day. He thought that because he had a German name the Operations officer who made the crew assignment must have doubted his loyalty to the Allied war effort and decided he should stay home.

Another friend in my squadron, after learning he was assigned to fly the mission, became very quiet and withdrawn. It turned out he had a premonition that he would be killed. His premonition was correct.

The Rhine Invasion was the last time gliders were used in an airborne assault. It proved too costly in men and material. Of the 600 that went in that day, only six were still flyable and could be salvaged."

We honor our veterans past and present for protecting freedom.

Only in America, God Bless it.

Chapter 44

A Free Nation Votes

I admit I held my figurative nose when I voted but I made a decision. I am only one voice but my vote counts exactly the same as the governor of the state or the President of the United States, no more, no less.

My polling place was an elementary school. Most of the ten booths were full, but I didn't have to wait in line. It was quiet, but there was a sense of excitement in the room. I marked an electronic ballot and tapped a button marked 'record my vote.'

This has been a long and bloody presidential campaign season. Civility was the first casualty. I'm glad it's over.

Our new president is the 44th president. Grover Cleveland sometimes gets counted twice and bumps the number up to 45 because he was elected in non-consecutive elections. The 2016 election was the 56th since the first when George Washington was elected president in 1788.

Before that time, the Articles of Confederation formalized after the Revolutionary War, determined that the Confederation Congress embodied the interstate government. It had a presiding officer, but he was not a chief executive.

The Constitution of the United States signed in 1788, required a chief executive. At first, each state was given a population-ratio number of electoral votes and each elector had two votes, one for president and one for vice president.

But those electoral votes were not specifically designated for each office. The man who won the most votes would be president and the man who won the second most votes would be vice president and president of the Senate.

George Washington won 69 of 69 first votes and John Adams received more of the second vote than any other of the eleven candidates. Sixteen years later an amendment to the Constitution changed the procedure so that votes were cast specifically for president and vice-president.

The two-party system is not a Constitutional requirement. It formed probably from the winner-take-all method used in conducting American elections. The two parties evolved and reshaped. First there were Federalists and Democratic-Republicans. Then the Democratic-Republican party split into Adams' Men and Jackson's Men. (referencing John Quincy Adams and Andrew Jackson)

Party names stopped evolving when Jackson's Men called themselves the Democratic party. Though the opposition supporting Adams called themselves the National Republicans, they would later be called Whigs, then Free Soil Party and finally in 1854 just Republicans. The Republican party was formed of those favoring abolishment of slavery, Whigs and Free Soilers.

Women were given the vote in 1920. Though Blacks were given the right to vote in 1870 by Federal law, it wasn't until 1965 that the Federal Government passed the Voting Rights Act which ensured that all living adult American citizens had equal access to vote, regardless of gender or ethnicity.

In the 2016 election, my husband Jeff was selected to fill out an exit poll. I had always wondered where demographic data on voting trends came from. I chatted with the exit pollsters. They were all college students, mostly political science majors. They explained that the purpose of the exit poll was not only to give impatient citizens an idea how the election was going, but to provide voting trends data. The questions on the poll included age, religion, gender, ethnicity, and ranking factors that influenced the voter's decision. The rest of the exit poll was a similar ballot to the one he had just filled out to be counted.

As I stood chatting, only one of the dozen or so people asked to participate declined. She had a child in a stroller and said she had to be somewhere to pick up another child.

Whether you or I are pleased or even minimally satisfied with the election results, it's a blessing and a privilege to be able to make our voices heard in safety and freedom.

Only in America, God bless it.

Son Daniel at George Washington's home, Mount Vernon

Chapter 45

George Washington, an Ordinary Hero

We remember George Washington for leading a rag-tag army against all odds with the outcome far from certain. If he failed to win independence, he would be tortured to death and his dead body mutilated. He believed wholeheartedly in the cause of freedom. Though his heart was in his thriving plantation and the agricultural experiments he loved, he was at last persuaded to become the general in pursuit of independence from the most powerful nation in the world. But Congress turned out to be as big of a foe. He was also viciously criticized for his errors in military judgement, (as detractors claimed) and disloyal politicians who believed him incompetent, tried to have him relieved of duty. The army shivered and starved while congress wrangled in rhetoric month after month.

The man George Washington was not the sort to seek or enjoy power. When independence was secure, Many Americans wanted George Washington to be the king of America. He vehemently declined. He had done his duty and he believed a monarchy would only destroy the new, dearly-won freedom.

He longed to go to his country home on the banks of the Potomac River. He had inherited the site from his brother and delighted in the science and order of farming. His diaries detailed the progress of crops and animals and provided him a basis for constant improvement.

He wrote in his journal that it "was the responsibility of wealthy farmers to undertake experimentation, as failures would be inevitable and losses would have to be absorbed while new techniques were perfected."

He had several farms as part of the Mt. Vernon estate. Though he started out growing tobacco, he switched to wheat because it was a more useful crop. Washington's 5,000 acre estate became one of the largest wheat growers in the country. He experimented with different varieties of wheat and learned to rotate his wheat with beans to replenish soil nutrients. He freely lectured small-land holders on increasing quality and yields.

Washington enjoyed developing clever new techniques that saved money and time. He was 'down to earth' in the literal sense.

 The house at Mt. Vernon was built in stages over a period of 20 years. Though he was a wealthy man, he liked to economize where he could. Though white stone facades were popular in that time, he opted for a faux finish to look like stone. He devised a method of throwing sand on wet plaster, troweling in the faux joints and once it was set, painting it.

Though the first president is often portrayed with a severe expression, he loved parties. He especially loved to dance and was known to be a talented partner.

 He was 6' 2" tall. An evening suit that was Washington's is on display at the Old Exchange in Charleston SC. Gauging from the suit, he was also extremely slender.

He probably didn't have wooden teeth, but he did have several sets made of exotic material. His journal notes chronic mouth pain from ill-fitting dentures. His cause of death at age 63 was epiglottitis. One of the doctors attending him wanted to perform a tracheotomy but was overruled. The procedure might have saved Washington's life. As he lay dying, he said he wanted a "decent burial" and not to be put into the earth in less than three days.

His wife Martha burned all of their private letters on the day of his death to protect their privacy. They were said to be happily married but produced no children, though she had children from her first marriage.

Like other folks with interests, weaknesses, and talents, George Washington became renown because he "more than self, his country loved."

Only in America, God Bless it.

Chapter 46

Get a Move On

We have a lot of stuff. Just stuff. It's the stuff that keeps lots of Americans anchored to a home. Moving our bodies is no big deal, but the trim and trappings of prosperity make for a mountain of belongings, and moving a mountain takes more than faith.

The pioneers were forced to leave most of their stuff. In many ways, it seems like a way of buying freedom. Before we had R.V's or moving vans, covered wagons hauled Americans on the move. But the movie version of a whole family riding along on the buckboard is pure fantasy.

Covered wagons were heavy when they were empty, and could carry only about a ton of stuff. A typical move took 5 months, and the wagon had to carry food, bedding, a tent and extra clothing at the very least. The foodstuff for one adult on the Oregon Trail amounted to about 400 pounds. About half that was flour with the rest being made up of salted meats dried fruit and vegetables, sugar, seasonings and leavening to make it palatable.

When the choice came down to food and shelter or fine furnishings or heirloom dishes, the choice wasn't too difficult. But when the choice was between heirloom dishes and riding on the wagon instead of walking, most people chose to walk. Part of the required pioneer equipment was an extra pair of shoes.

My husband and I recently undertook a major move. An internet search showed that we would save something in the neighborhood of $20,000 by doing it ourselves. That's because of the volume of our stuff. We think we need different clothes for different seasons, different dishes for different holidays and furniture designed to stay in one place instead of being moved from room to room as need requires.

 In my own defense, I gave away at least 100 books, a couch, a dresser, a sideboard, and curio cabinet . I also gave away about a ton of food storage, several dozen empty and full mason jars, and loads of bedding, towels and home décor. I knew I needed to whittle down my stuff.

 I have no idea how many tons of stuff we moved in our two 26' rented trucks. They were packed like a brain-puzzle, with every niche and gap stuffed with something, fitted and wedged to provide stability.

We made two trips with my husband driving the truck and me following along behind in a car. On the first load, the truck box

listed noticeably to the right because none of us thought to balance the weight in the load. Among our treasures is a 1903 upright piano. It weighs about a half a ton. It takes a minimum of four adults using a dolly to wrestle it in and out of a moving truck. It was on the same side as loads of books and other heavy items that happened to fit.

We stored the first load in a storage unit, expecting to take our time shopping for a new home. But we found it quickly and closed three weeks later.

After two grueling drives fueled by enough caffeine to make a rock jittery, we pulled up to our new house and rolled open the gate. Our stuff was (mostly) all safe. Our new neighbors started showing up to introduce themselves, answer questions and help us unload. We felt instantly welcome and our house seemed more like home every moment.

I don't think I need all the stuff we moved. But I am grateful that I can choose to keep or discard stuff according to my own priorities.

Only in America, God Bless it!

Beth Stephenson

Chapter 47

Neighborhoods Festooned with Ribbons

I got a notice from our old neighborhood today that there's a rabid squirrel terrorizing the neighborhood. Someone has already trapped it and is waiting for the game warden to diagnose and remove it.

 Lost dogs and cats are also quickly retrieved through a kind neighborhood network. Even the birth of new fawns each spring is announced via emails. Though I'm not there anymore, it still tickles me to read the neighborly warnings to protect humans and pets and even wildlife in that little Oklahoma community.

Heartbreak has touched my own family in recent weeks. My nephew and his wife eagerly anticipated the birth of their second child. Their cute little boy was looking forward to being a good big brother to the little sister due before Thanksgiving.

The mother wanted to have an un-medicated birth and planned to deliver in a hospital with the assistance of a midwife and a doula (or labor coach).

The last appointment before her due date went fine. Baby was robust, Mom was healthy.

A week later, labor came on fast and strong. The midwife arrived but there was no time to get to the hospital. The paramedics assisted in the delivery. But the baby didn't breathe. The perfectly-formed little girl had no heartbeat.

The paramedics rushed her via ambulance to the hospital while trying to elicit some sign of life. But it was not to be. Doctors determined that the baby girl had died a couple of days before birth. No amount of resuscitation or intervention would have helped.

The little family spent a few hours in the hospital, holding the wee body, examining every inch to make memories to last their lifetimes. Grandparents drove through the night to join with them in grieving.

The broken hearted parents drove home from the hospital the next day without the pink bundle they had anticipated for so long. As they turned off the main road into their Saratoga Springs, Utah neighborhood, they noticed a pink ribbon on the light post. The

nearby tree had one too. Grosgrain and satin, bright pink and soft, baby pink: ribbons were everywhere. Not only their street but for several blocks in every direction, the posts and pillars and trees and bushes and anything else was adorned with pink ribbon. Their own house was festooned with pink tulle. Tulle is the stuff of ballerina dresses and Easter petticoats.

I'm sure that some of the neighbors wondered if their gesture would be more painful than comforting. But they had to do something. How could anyone misinterpret such a gesture of love?

The following days were tearful and grief-filled. Neighbors and members of their church congregation stopped quietly by to drop off meals and treats and to take care of their physical needs. Their home with flowers like a summer garden.

Someone handed out Forget-Me-Not seed packets at the brief funeral service.

Sometimes the ribbons are yellow. Sometimes they are red, white and blue. But they always mean neighbors are loving neighbors. It's part of our American tradition.

Only in America, God bless it.

Chapter 48

On Thanksgiving

I am thankful for food. I'm grateful for the weight problem I have to constantly monitor because of the abundance of tasty, nutritious, inexpensive, culinary choices.

The traditions of the Thanksgiving holiday all point subtly to the celebration of American abundance.

Nutritionists may rightly tell us that too much of a good thing ceases to be a good thing, but how blessed our beltlines are that we can choose what, when and how much we eat because of the great prosperity in this nation.

There are hungry people, true. But it is an extremely rare adult that has no access to food if they are willing to seek it.

The pilgrims of Plymouth, Massachusetts celebrated the harvest with their Wampanoag Indian neighbors. The feast went on for three days but only one menu item is known for certain. The Indians brought five deer as a gift to the settlers.

What we don't know from positive records of the 1621 celebration, we can surmise. Wildfowl are mentioned in old journals as having been part of the feast, and turkeys are abundant in that area. Fish and shellfish were also a staple of the pilgrims' diet.

The venison would likely have been cut into chunks and roasted on a spit and the wildfowl may have been roasted on an open fire or boiled with vegetables in a stew.

Corn was almost certainly part of the menu, but only the savory type ground into meal. Pumpkins were also likely participants, but they would have been served as a vegetable and certainly not creamed, sweetened and served as a custard pie.

Cranberries, melons, wild grapes and plums are native to New England and almost certainly made it to the Thanksgiving feast. Apple trees are not native and though they had probably been planted would not be mature enough to produce for several more years.

We don't know what common English vegetables had been planted and produced well those first years, but native vegetables like wild onions and Jerusalem artichoke tubers probably made an appearance.

Things have changed. Earlier this year I was on a nature bog hike

near the West Virginia and Maryland border. We enjoyed picking wild blackberries and blueberries but as we got onto the board walk, I was too suspicious of the little roundish berries growing low over the mossy surface of the water to pick, let alone taste them. Only when we were almost finished with the boggy part did I realize that I had seen my first wild cranberries. I broke one open and verified that it was indeed the famous Thanksgiving species. I'd made whole-berry cranberry sauce for thirty years but didn't recognize it in its natural state.

I'm sure I'm not alone. It's a rare person who knows how to dress game for roasting. How many Americans will dig potatoes and sweet potatoes in the backyard garden in preparation for their feast? Most Americans would never think to save their Halloween Jack-o-lantern for their Thanksgiving pumpkin pie. (I do.)

I wish I could invite a Pilgrim to my Thanksgiving feast. How fun would it be to show him the eight varieties of pies and the array of soft, warm rolls, jams, casseroles, meats and eats of which he never dreamed. The abundance we enjoy would astonish and overwhelm him.

Only in America, God Bless it.

I didn't recognize the wild cranberries at first.

Chapter 49

Yellowstone, Our First National Park

I wasn't ready to be awestruck by one of America's most famous natural wonders. But Old Faithful in Yellowstone National Park, Wyoming doesn't wait around for tourists to gather or lens caps to come off. But we didn't worry. Old Faithful geyser got its name for a reason.

Ulysses S Grant signed a bill setting aside Yellowstone as America's first national park. 2.2 million acres of geothermic sites, deep gorges, rivers, lakes, forests and breathtaking vistas belong to the citizens of the USA.

I last visited there about seventeen years ago. A huge fire had scrubbed out the bark beetle and mistletoe about 10 years before. The region bristled with young trees like masculine chins at the end of No-Shave November.

Park rangers assured us that a fire was anything but a natural disaster. Once in a while, nature needs a new start so that disease and infestations are stopped and the ecosystem can shift upward again.

Buffalo and elk wander the flower-strewn valleys. We didn't see any of the park's famous grizzly bears, but they're still there. The buffalo are accustomed to tourists, but signs are posted everywhere to avoid them entirely, if possible.

At one point, we got out of our car to hike down a boardwalk to see a geyser. The buffalo ignored the signs warning about the dangerous ground and treacherous footing. A huge buffalo with bloodshot eyes and fully developed horns and hump decided to make use of the boardwalk too and trotted toward us.

We had nowhere to go! We were scared to step off the path and afraid to flee. The buffalo paid no attention to us trembling tourists and sauntered over to graze the meadow near our car. We were trapped there awhile longer as we waited for him to wander far enough that we could safely get back into our car.

There is much more than geysers in Yellowstone. I was intrigued by a mud pot that roiled and boiled in a natural caldron. Morning Glory pool is one of the loveliest places in the park. A brilliant aqua-blue hot spring is surrounded with bright sulfuric yellow. The boardwalk is placed so that visitors can gaze deep into the deep, hot vent.

We had seen Old Faithful spew as we pulled into the parking lot, so we left it for last that day. Tourists gathered on the walks, sitting on the benches as the time neared. We waited almost 70 minutes, but we were well rewarded with the natural spectacle.

The intervals have changed over the years. In 1939, it averaged just over an hour. Earthquakes have adjusted the flow of water and now Old Faithful averages eruptions every 90 minutes. If the eruption lasts less than 2.5 minutes, the interval will be about an hour. If the eruption lasts more than 2.5 minutes, the next eruption will be expected about 90 minutes later.

Eruptions shoot between 4,000 gallons and 8,000 gallons of boiling water to an average height of 145 feet in the air.

Old Faithful, Morning Glory hot spring, and a host of other geothermic sites as well as gloriously beautiful and wild scenery will ever be part of our American legacy, thanks to the National parks system.

Only in America, God Bless it.

Old Faithful Geyser

My son Daniel in front of Morning Glory Pool

Chapter 50

White Elephants, Naughty or Nice

Tis the season for lots of holiday festivities, but one of the most popular American traditions has its roots far across the sea. Not in Bethlehem, nor any other middle eastern region, but in the Far East.

I had never heard this tradition called anything but a 'White Elephant Party' until I moved to Oklahoma where some folks call it 'Dirty Santa.' The concept is the same. Here are the rules.

Each guest brings some sort of useless oddity wrapped as a gift. Each one draws a number from a hat that determines which order they get to choose. The first person chooses a gift from the pile and unwraps it. The next participant has the option of taking something that is already unwrapped or choosing something to unwrap themselves.

If they choose something that is already unwrapped, the person they take from may then choose to unwrap something else or to steal somebody else's gift. We always put a limit on the number of times a gift can change hands to avoid the party lasting all night.

There are always a few too nice to truly get into the spirit of the game. They bring lovely glove and scarf sets, pretty scented candles, or good-quality chocolates.

Then there are those that enjoy the devilish pleasure of finding the ultimate white elephant. Last year, I gave a reddish wig. I had noticed my hair was thinning, and had ordered a few wigs online to try out. The thing looked like it was fresh off of Ginger's head from Gilligan's Island. A man from our Church who is totally bald opened the wig and nobody took it from him.

The concept of the gift of a white elephant originates in ancient Siam, now Thailand. Albino elephants were sacred symbols of a monarch's power and wealth. White elephants were protected by law and could not be used for work. Creative rulers realized the inconvenience of such a possession and are said to have awarded the white elephants to courtiers that became obnoxious. The expense of keeping such a behemoth and receiving no benefit from it would soon ruin the annoying person and they would leave the court.

P.T. Barnum is said to have brought the tradition to the west when he imported a "sacred white" elephant at great expense and trouble, only to find that it was really light grey with pink spots.

Now any expensive thing or project that turns out to be useless is dubbed a white elephant. Certain airports, malls, and wedding gifts have received the title.

Yet even white elephants can be enjoyed. Last year, we ended up with festive toilet paper and a bottle of poo-pourri. Instructions say to drop a few drops of the poo-pourri into the toilet and it prevents odors from spreading. Ingenious! Who would give that away?

Ugly jewelry, giant brass insects, wig manikins, ugly Christmas tree ornaments, fruitcake, a hotdog, too-small lingerie, and outdated clothing have also made appearances at white elephant parties. A white porcelain elephant figurine traded owners at the annual party every year we lived in Colorado.

The trick is to remember what you receive from whom. It's important to avoid re-gifting as white elephants items you received with gentle intent from others that may attend the party.

Though not strictly an American tradition, white elephants are a delightfully dubious part of our holidays.

Only in America, God bless it.

Chapter 51

A Right Jolly Old Elf

There's truth in every legend.

St. Nicolas is a real saint. He was also a third-fourth century Turk. The earliest stories relating to Nicolas say that he gave away his inheritance to the poor and the needy. One version of the legend says that he gave three bags of gold or three gold balls to a poor man with three daughters. The tradition of an orange in the toe of a stocking hearkens back to the gold balls or bags of gold given by the saint.

After his death on Dec 6 in AD 343, some effusion from the soil of his grave was named "manna." The liquid was said to have healing properties, and contributed to his candidacy to Sainthood. Centuries after his death, miracles of rescue and calming seas after praying to St. Nicolas made him the patron saint of children, gift seekers, and sailors as well as almost any other person in trouble.

But St. Nicolas, still revered as a saint by the current Catholic Church and other related denominations, is quite a far cry from the "right jolly old elf" we associate with the Christmas season.

The American Santa started with a lengthy poem, by Clement Clark Moore, a professor of Oriental and Greek literature, Divinity and Biblical Learning at the General Theological Seminary of the Episcopal Church in New York City. Titled 'A Visit from St. Nicolas', it is better known as 'Twas the Night Before Christmas.'

The poem was published anonymously in 1823. As the son of an Episcopal Bishop, Moore was first anxious about the whimsical note he attached to a bona fide saint. When it was wildly popular, he apparently decided it wasn't much of a threat to Christian piety.

Twas the Night Before Christmas introduced an elf dressed in fur, (a product supplied almost exclusively by the USA at that time,) who rides in a magical sleigh pulled by reindeer. Moore explained Santa's access to children's shoes and stockings by his magical ability to slide down the ubiquitous chimney opening. His long white beard and his rotund body are also the product of Moore's poem.

In 1881, Thomas Nast, a cartoonist for the magazine *Harper's Weekly,* drew on Moore's poem when he drew Santa Claus as we expect him to look now. The red and white of his suit hearkens to the traditional religious vestments of the original Saint. As Nast continued to depict Santa, he added the work shop in the North Pole, the elves and the Naughty and Nice list.

A lengthy poem by Robert L. May, a copywriter for the Montgomery Ward Department store, introduced Rudolf the Red-Nosed Reindeer in 1939. The storybook sold 6 million copies over 7 years.

Though other countries adhere to the tradition of gift giving at Christmas time, their traditions include a Christmas Angel in Italy. Kris Kringle, (or Christkind) brings gifts to lucky German and Swiss children. Babouschka in Russia is an old woman who is said to have misdirected the three wise men on purpose. Later, she repented of her misdeed and now on January 6, she places goodies in children's shoes and stockings, hoping that she can find the Christ Child. Scandinavian children look for Jultomten, who delivers treats carried in a sleigh drawn by goats.

Our fat, jolly Santa Claus is as American as Uncle Sam and Lady Liberty. But as an American, I'm going to make sure I'm on the Nice list, just in case.

Only in America, God bless it.

Clement Clark Moore's "A Visit from St. Nicholas" is better known as "Twas the Night Before Christmas"

Chapter 52

Charitable Giving

Ah, the last week of the year! We wake up on the 26th from our long winter's nap and realize that tax season is about to start. We have just a few days to finish with last year's resolutions. And the holiday sweets are shunted aside in favor of salty New Year's (read Bowl Game Day) snacks.

But back to the taxes. This is the week to give birth if you can. A child born just one minute before midnight on Dec 31st qualifies for the child tax credit.

Take a peek at your total family income for the year and check out the potential tax bracket. Is it possible that giving a little more will actually benefit your annual bottom line?

Whatever your motive, Americans give a lot of money to charities. According to tax records for those who itemized deductions for 2015, 67% of itemizers gave some money to charity. Givers gave twice as much to religious organizations as to secular organizations. 34% of those givers gave both to religious and secular charitable organizations.

These statistics don't take into consideration those who don't make enough to justify itemizing their taxes. Those at the top and bottom of the income scale give a much higher percentage of their income than the middle income earners. If the trend holds true, it's safe to assume that non-itemizers give generously also.

The mailbox becomes a guilt buffet as it offers an array of charitable organizations that desperately need my help. Who can drop a plea from the children's hospital in the trash? There are animals needing care, there are hungry and cold and homeless people on the streets in our town. Less than two bucks supplies a hearty holiday meal. The school bands want to travel, the boy scouts and the girl scouts want to help our youth. There are the beggars that claim to be in immediate need.

Then there are tithes and offerings at our local churches. Will a man rob God? Volunteers ring the bells for the Salvation Army's red buckets.

We have a holiday tradition of watching the movie "A Christmas Carol" each year. The lines from Scrooge before-the-ghosts' visits, like Christmas bells in our ears. "Are there no work houses…?" I fill in "no homeless shelters, no housing projects, no food stamps?"

Scrooge is assured that they are still in full force. "They cost enough…" he says.

The solicitors answer, "Some cannot go there and some would rather die."

Scrooge: "If they would rather die, let them do so and decrease the surplus population."

Am I as hopeless as Scrooge if I drop most of pleas in the trash?

Millions of Americans use websites like Charity Navigator to see which charities manage their donations best. Such sites disclose how much goes to overhead, salaries, etc. and how much actually benefits the needy or cause.

There is a dramatic difference in "generosity index" by state. Generally speaking, according to Philanthropy.com, the more religiously active or politically conservative a state is, the higher the percentage of charitable givers including volunteerism. Utah has the highest percentage of charitable givers and New Hampshire has the lowest. Oklahoma ranks eighth.

Regardless of the regional statistics, Americans are generous. Part of our national heritage is to care for the less fortunate. The final reckoning of the tax year is a good time to beef up the blessings.

Only in America, God Bless it.

ABOUT THE AUTHOR

Other than *Americana*

Beth M. Stephenson writes historical fiction and moonlights as a travel writer. Her blog is www.ChocolateCreamCenters.com She's married to Jeff and together they have seven children, a girl and six boys.

Now that her children are raised, she has undertaken a quest to write the world into a better place.

When she's taking a break from writing, you'll find her travelling, reading, puttering in her garden or tinkering in her kitchen.

Beth has a Bachelor's Degree in English and American Literature from Brigham Young University. She and he husband have recently moved to Saratoga Springs, UT.